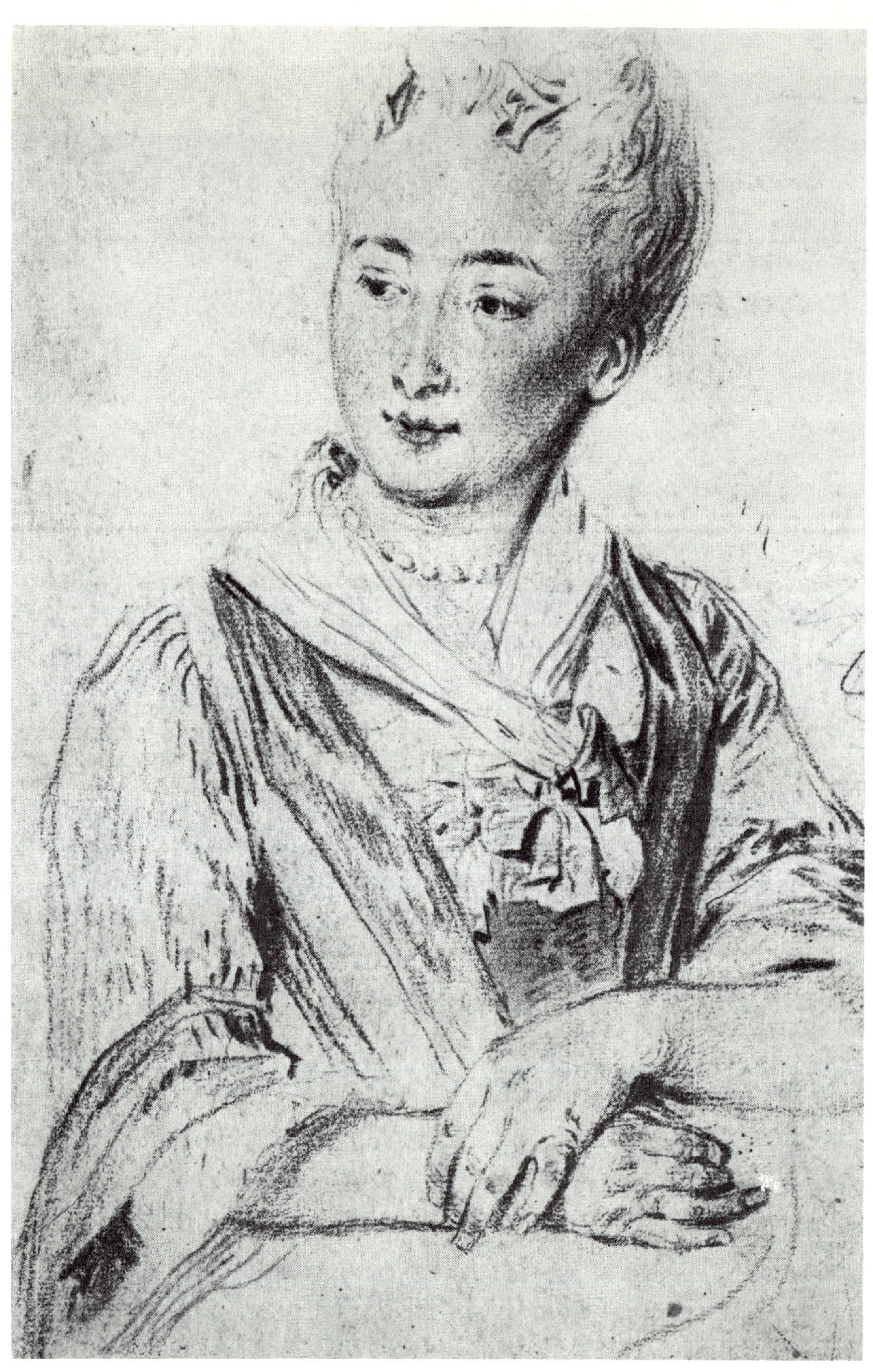

Young woman. Black and red chalk; 260 × 140 mm.

WATTEAU
DRAWINGS

44 Plates by

ANTOINE WATTEAU

Dover Publications, Inc., New York

PUBLISHER'S NOTE

Antoine Watteau was born in 1684 in Valenciennes, France. He early showed an inclination to sketch public performers—a sign of what was to come. He studied art locally but, at 18, decided to try his luck in Paris. Watteau soon joined the studio of the stage designer and decorator Claude Gillot (1673–1722), whose influence further developed his theatrical approach. After a break with Gillot—the cause of which has never been revealed—Watteau entered the studio of Claude Audran III, gaining access to the paintings in the Luxembourg, most notably those by Rubens. The artist later formed a friendship with the wealthy Pierre Crozat, who owned a collection of Flemish and Italian paintings. Exposure to all these works helped to form Watteau's style.

The artist had briefly returned to Valenciennes, but quickly returned to Paris and established his reputation. He was accepted by the Académie and secured favor and patronage for his airy depictions of *fêtes galantes*, theatrical troupes and scenes marked by their sense of the ephemeral (perhaps a result of his own precarious health). He died of tuberculosis on July 18, 1721.

Although Watteau is best known for paintings such as *L'embarquement pour l'île de Cythère*, *Gilles* and *L'enseigne de Gersaint*, his drawings share the same characteristics that mark the canvases: a theatrical presence, lightness of touch and a pervasive feeling of melancholy engendered by the realization that all pleasure is transitory. The drawings reflect Watteau's primary themes, including graceful women, characters from commedia dell'arte and Parisian street types. Some were studies for future works (such as the couple on page 43, who figure prominently in *L'embarquement pour l'île de Cythère*); others were not developed further. If occasional passages betray lapses of draftsmanship, the drawings are nevertheless remarkable in their poetry, spontaneity and immediacy.

The captions list subject, medium and dimensions (in millimeters, height before width).

Published in Canada by General Publishing Company, Ltd., 30 Lesmill Road, Don Mills, Toronto, Ontario.

Published in the United Kingdom by Constable and Company, Ltd., 10 Orange Street, London WC2H 7EG.

This Dover edition, first published in 1985, is a selection of plates from the portfolio *Antoine /Watteau / Cinquante-deux reproductions de Léon Marotte choisies par Charles / Martine, publiées avec un Catalogue raisonné par Émile Dacier, / Conservateur adjoint à la Bibliothèque nationale*, published as number X in the series *Dessins de Maîtres Français* by Helleu et Sergent, Éditeurs, Paris, 1930, in a limited edition of 360. The captions are based on the text by Dacier; a new Publisher's Note has been written specially for the present edition.

Manufactured in the United States of America
Dover Publications, Inc., 31 East 2nd Street, Mineola, N.Y. 11501

Library of Congress Cataloging in Publication Data

Watteau, Antoine, 1684–1721.
Watteau drawings.

(Dover art library)
"Selection of plates from the portfolio, Antoine Watteau : cinquante-deux reproductions de Léon Marotte choisies par Charles Martine, publiées avec un catalogue raisonné par Émile Dacier"—Verso of t.p.
1. Watteau, Antoine, 1684–1721—Catalogues raisonnés. I. Title. II. Series.
NC248.W3A4 1985 741.944 85-10408
ISBN 0-486-24958-1

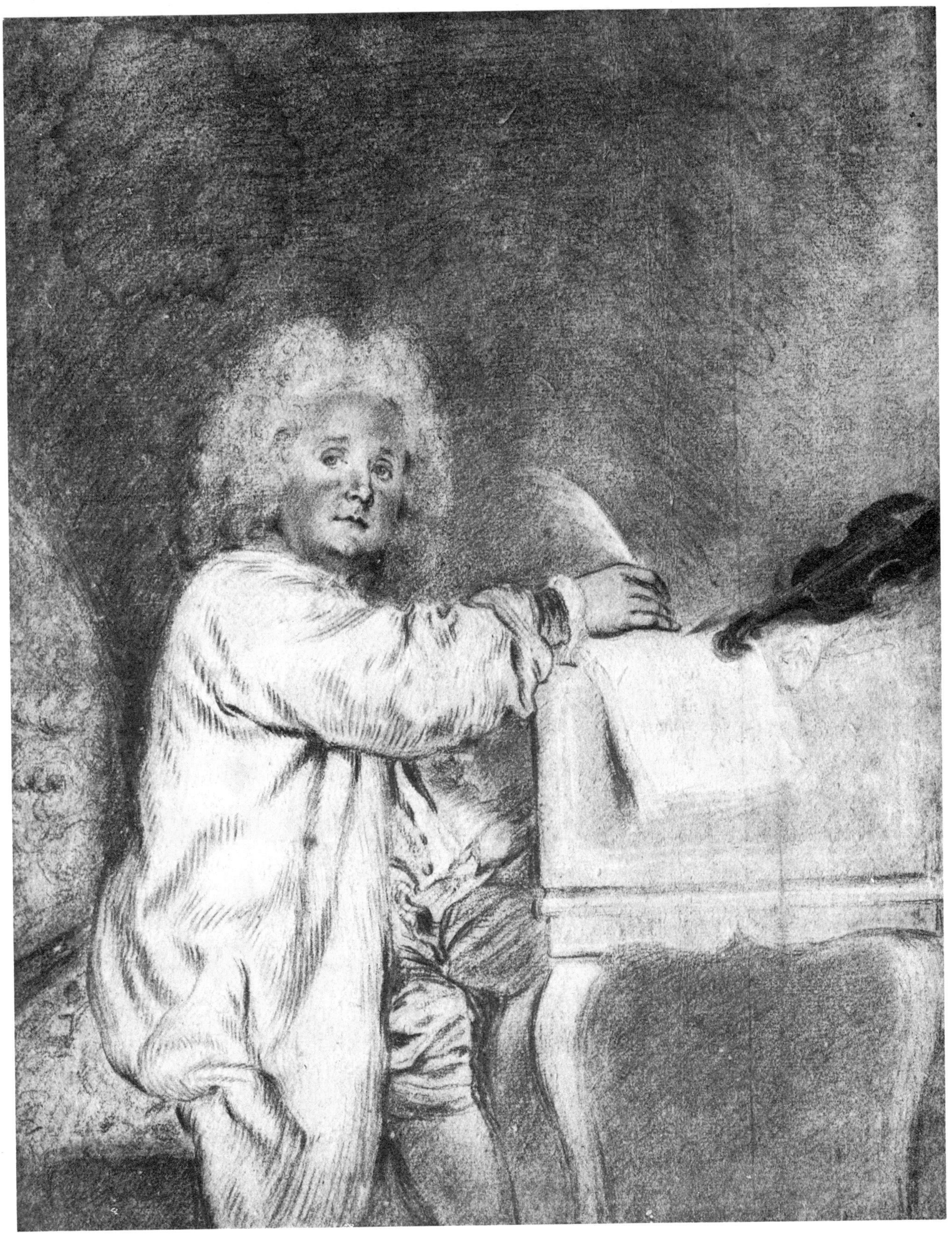

The composer Jean-Féry Rebel (1666–1747). Black, red and white chalk, background rubbed with black; 460 × 350 mm.

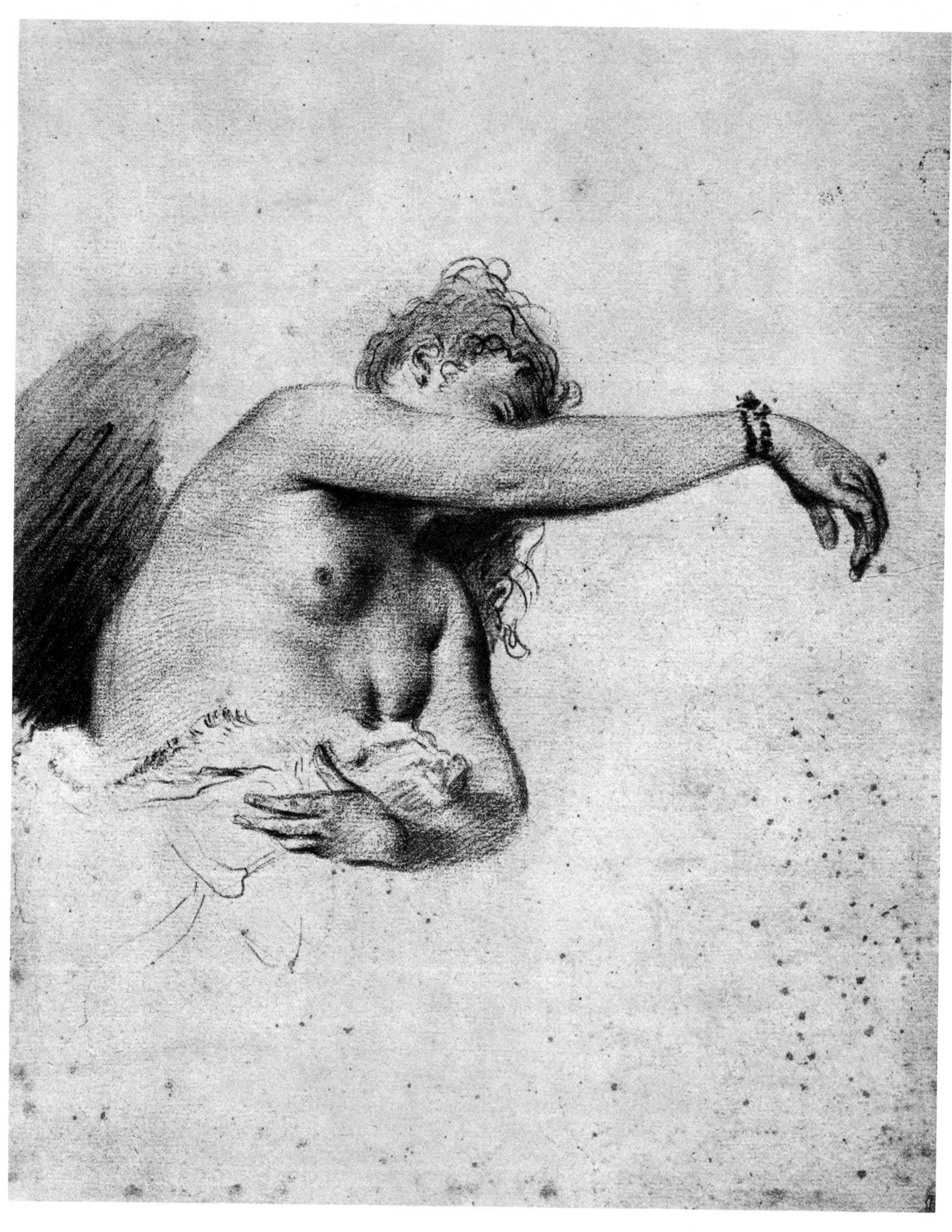

Young female nude. Red and black chalk; 283 × 233 mm.

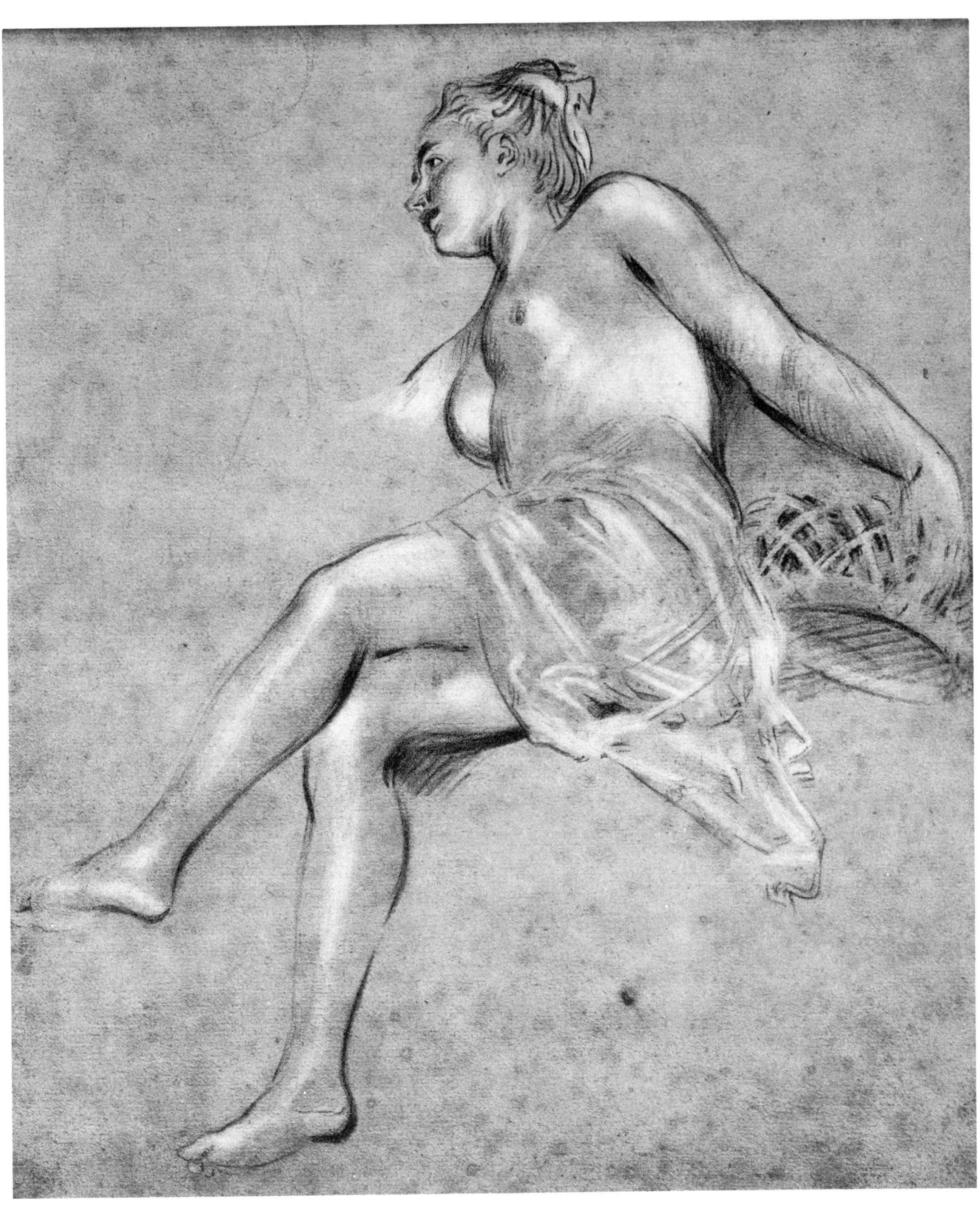

Study for *Spring* (one of a series, *The Seasons*, no longer extant). Black, red and white chalk on buff-colored paper; 324 × 277 mm.

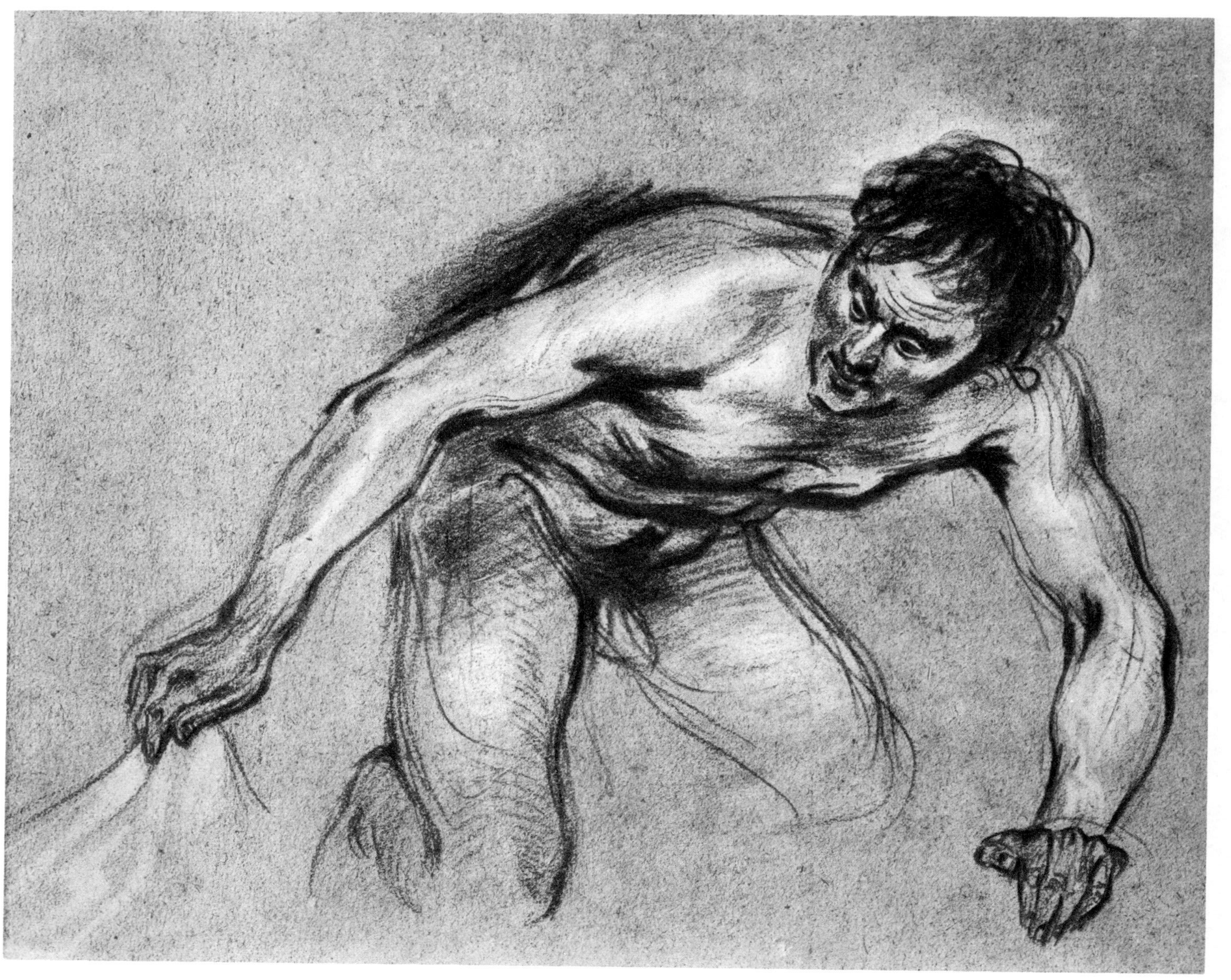

Male nude. Black, red and white chalk on gray paper; 245 × 298 mm.

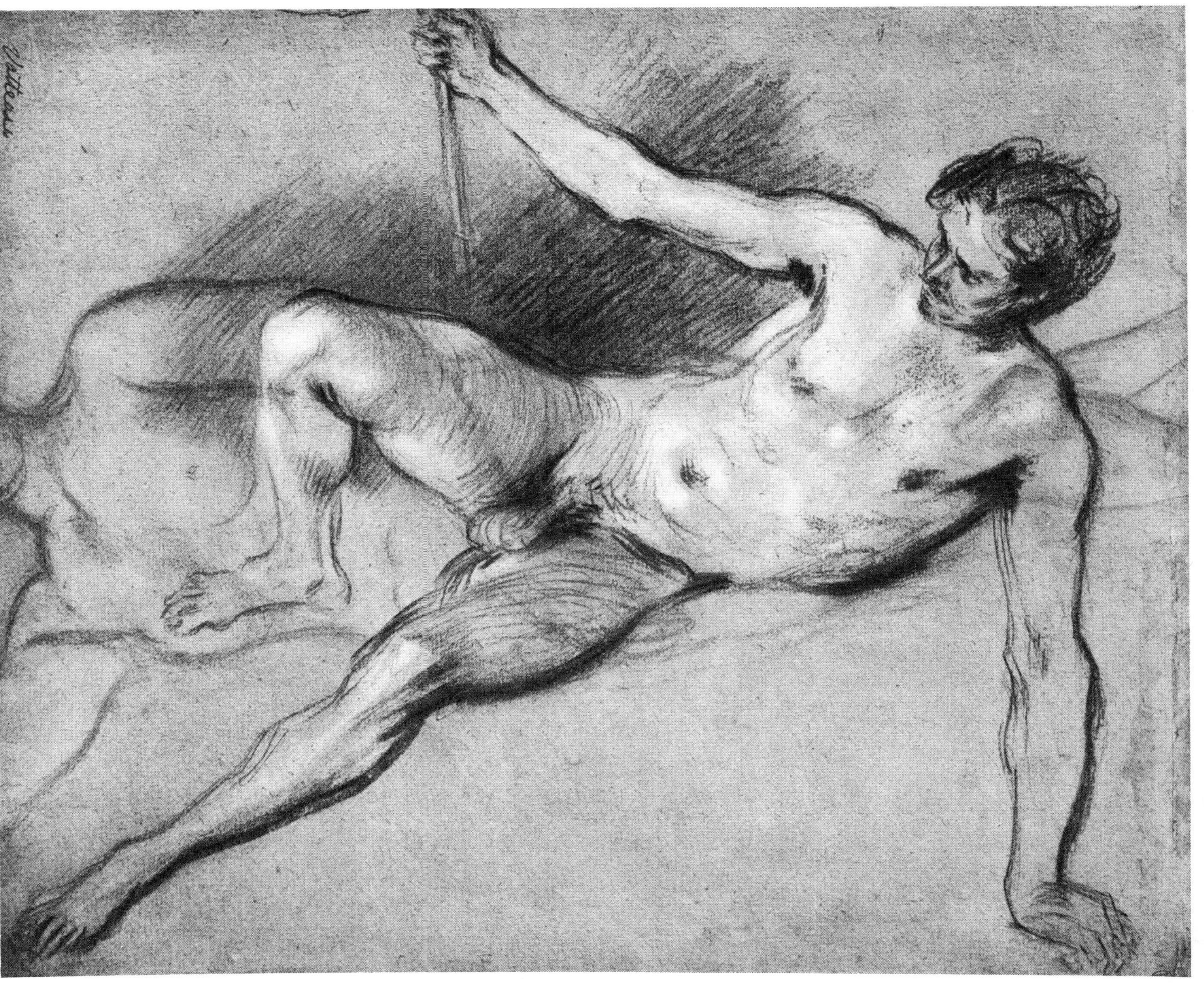

Male nude (drawn over a study of a female nude). Red, black and white chalk on yellowish-gray paper; 269 × 315 mm.

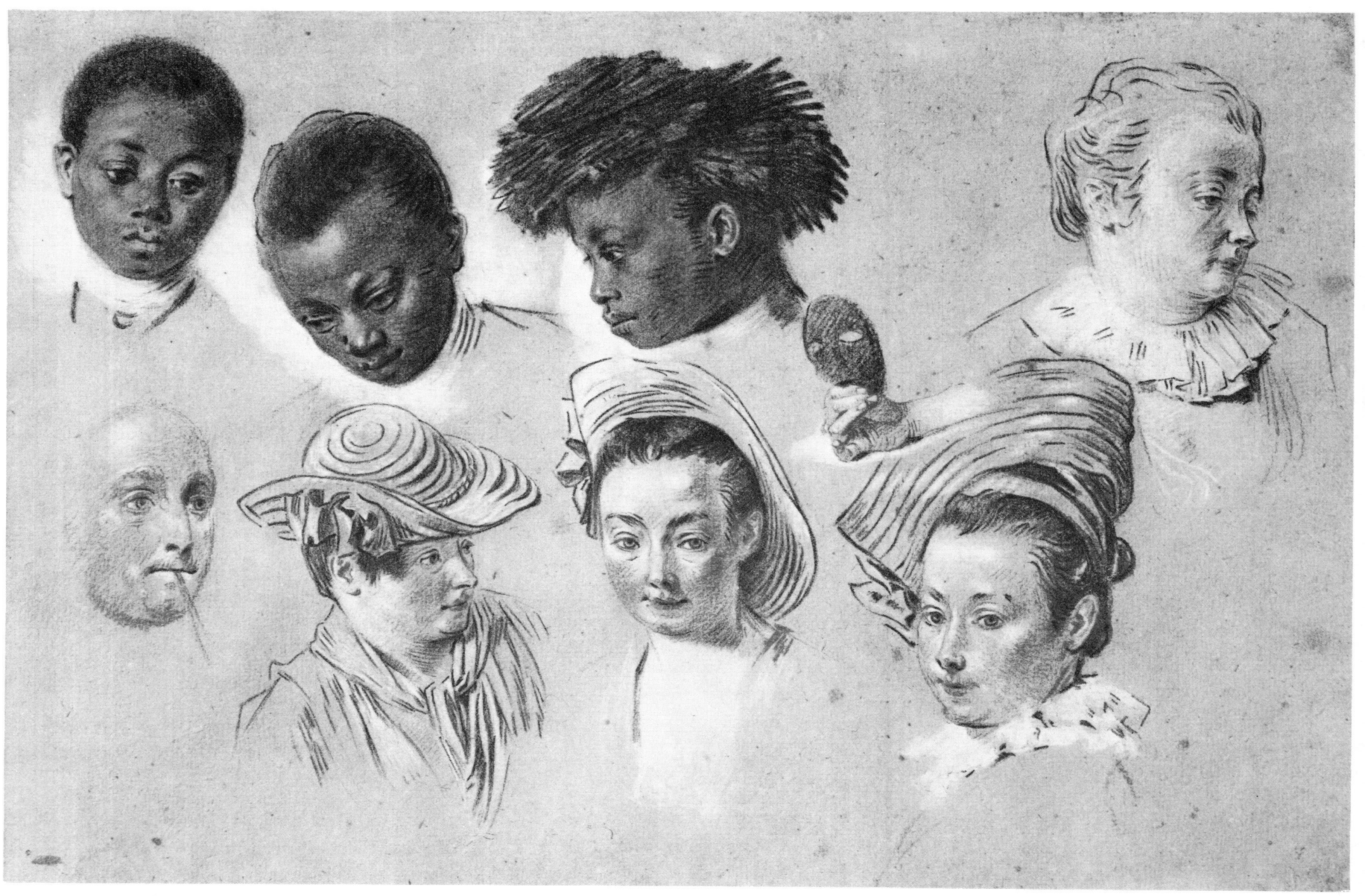

Eight heads (three of young blacks, one of a woman wearing a ruff, three of a woman wearing a large straw hat and one of a man) and a study of a right hand holding a mask. Red, black and white chalk; 267 × 397 mm.

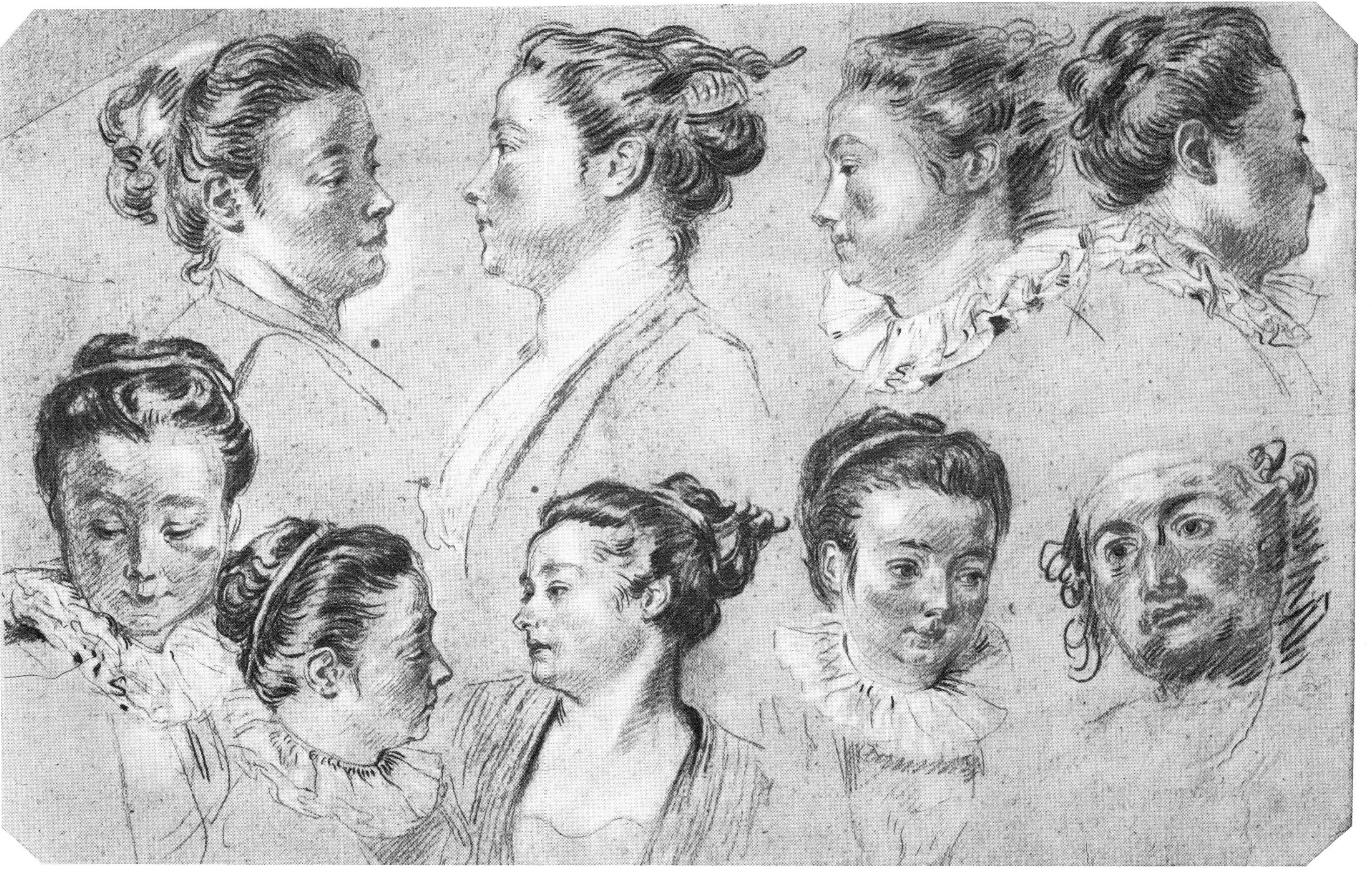

Nine heads (eight of women, one cf a man). Red, black and white chalk on gray paper; 250 × 381 mm.

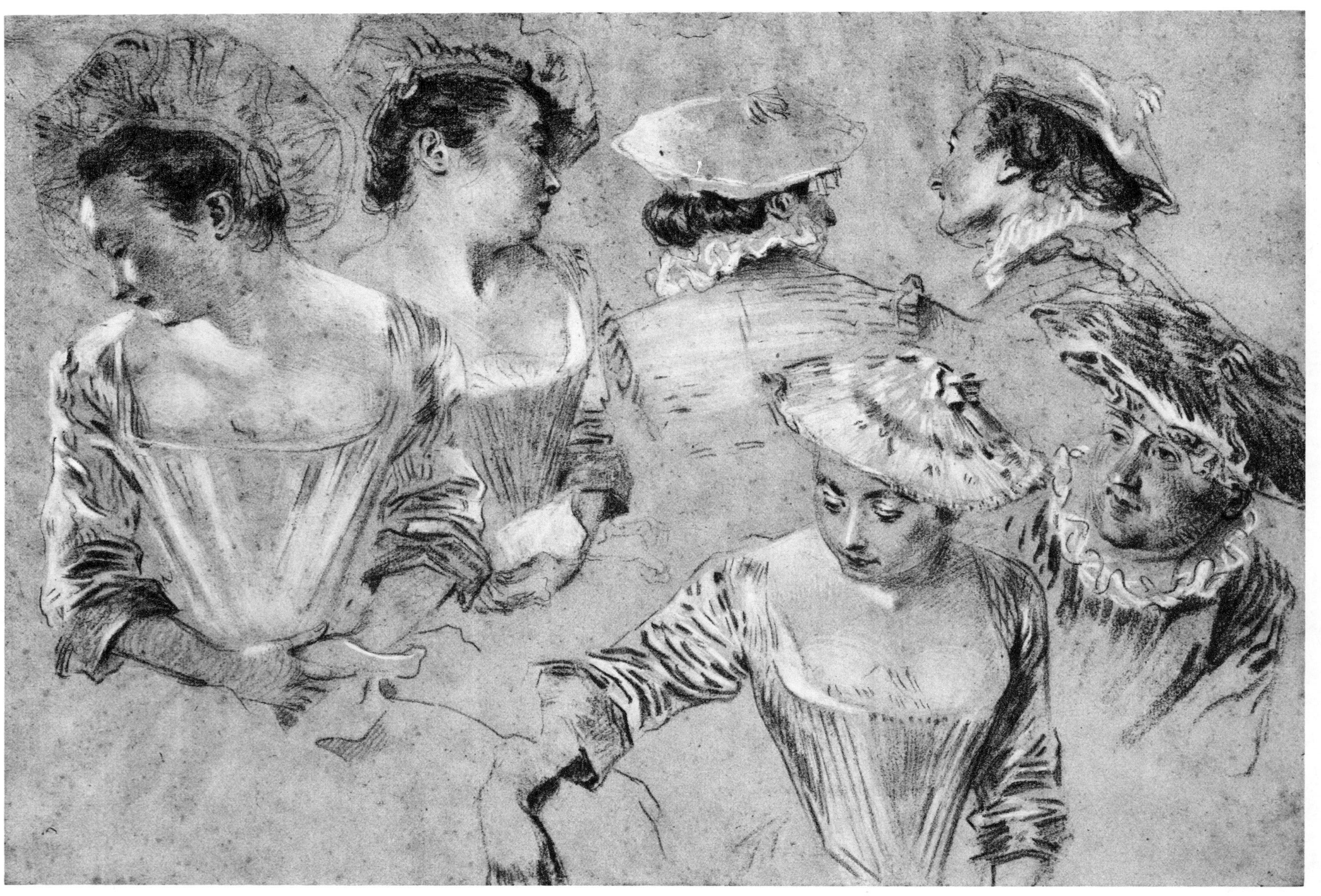

Three young women wearing a large gathered cap; the heads of three men in similar caps. Black, red and white chalk on gray paper; 270 × 380 mm.

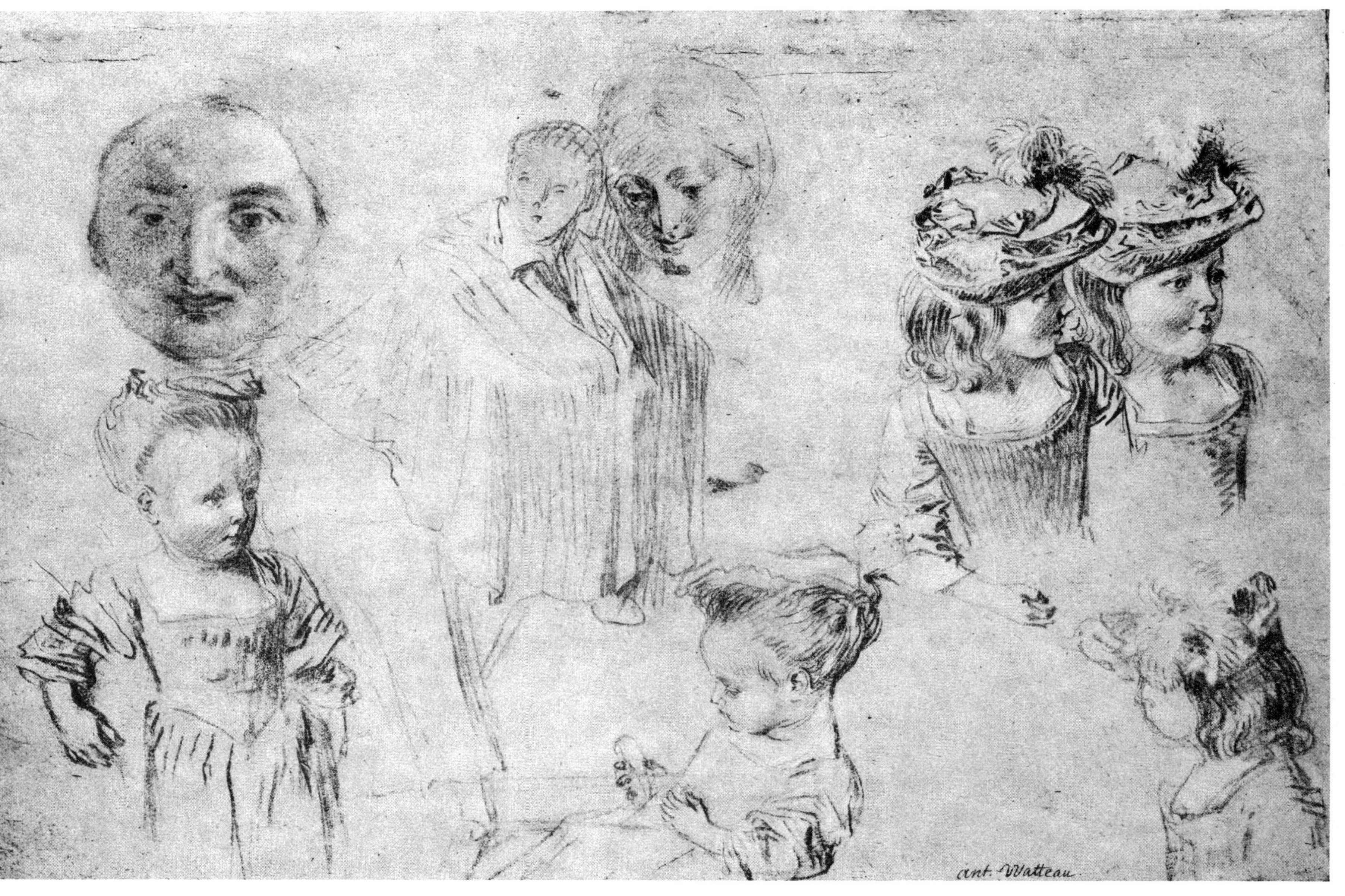

Head of Pierrot; figure of a standing man wrapped in a cloak, head of a woman, slightly bowed; three studies of a girl wearing a plumed hat; two studies of a child. Red and white chalk on gray paper; 271 × 400 mm.

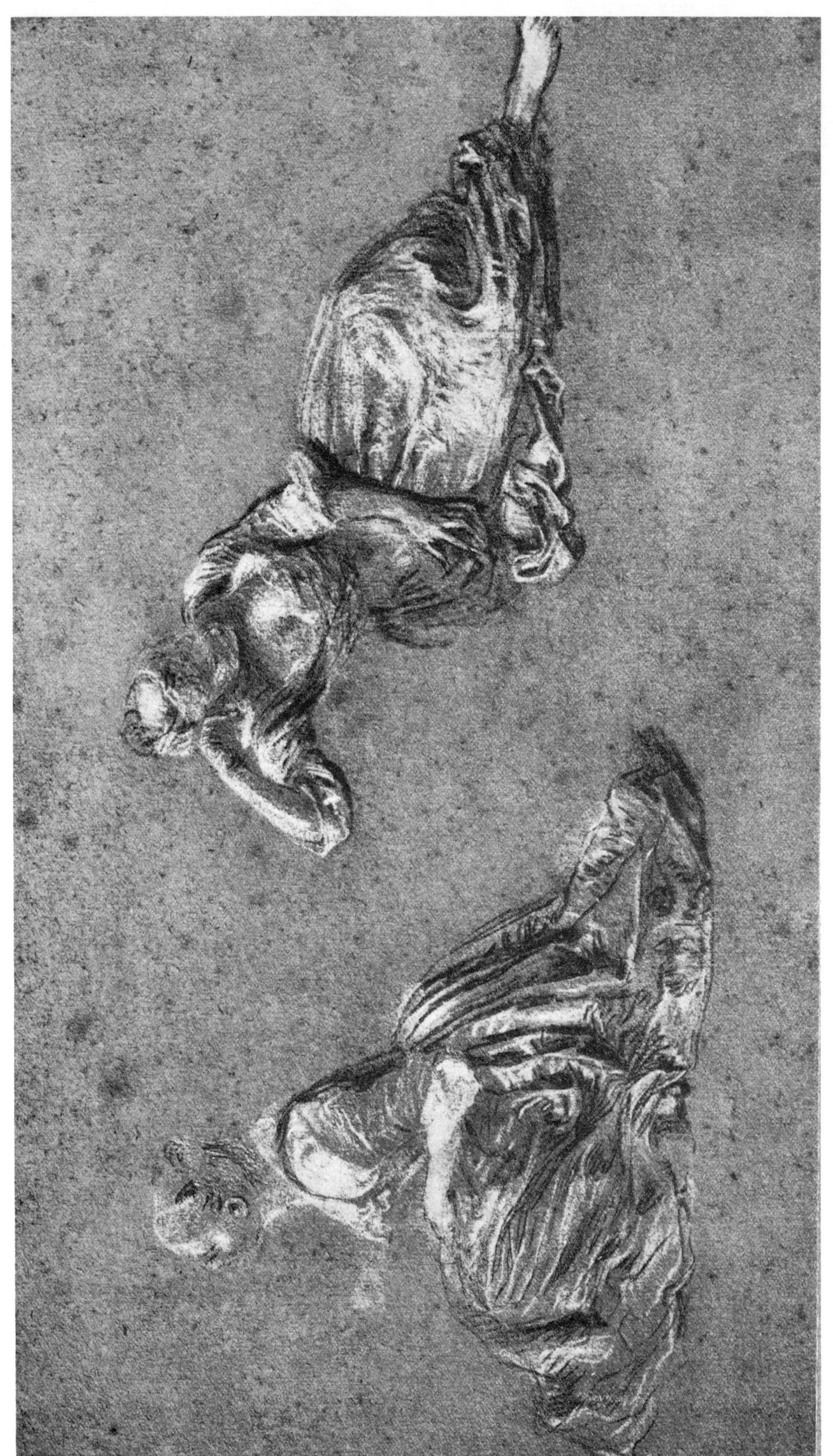

Two women. Black, red and white chalk and black lead on gray paper; 212 × 352 mm.

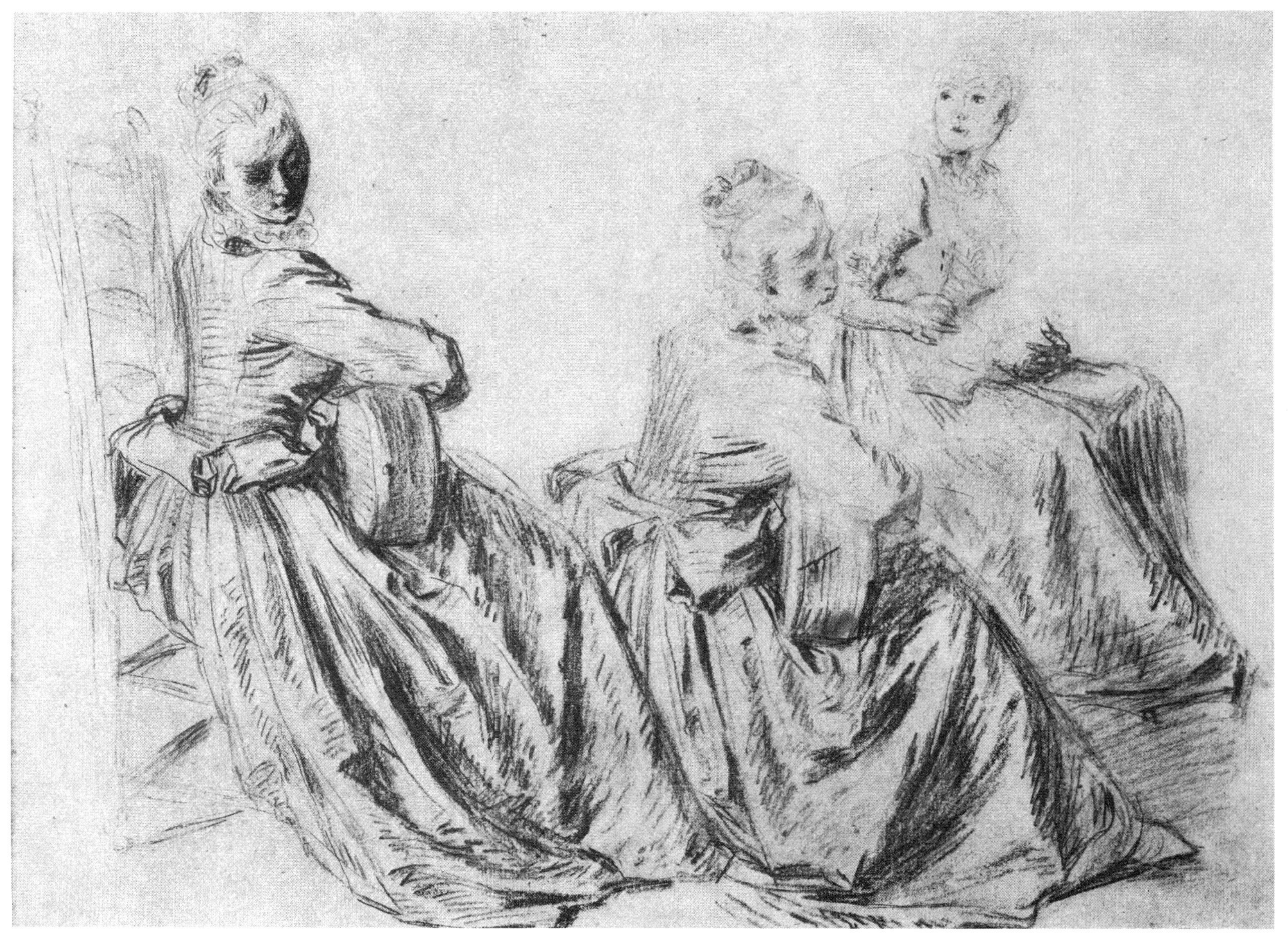

Three women, two playing the guitar and one holding a music book. Black chalk, with touches of red in the faces, the dress on the left and the hands of the right figure; 230 × 290 mm.

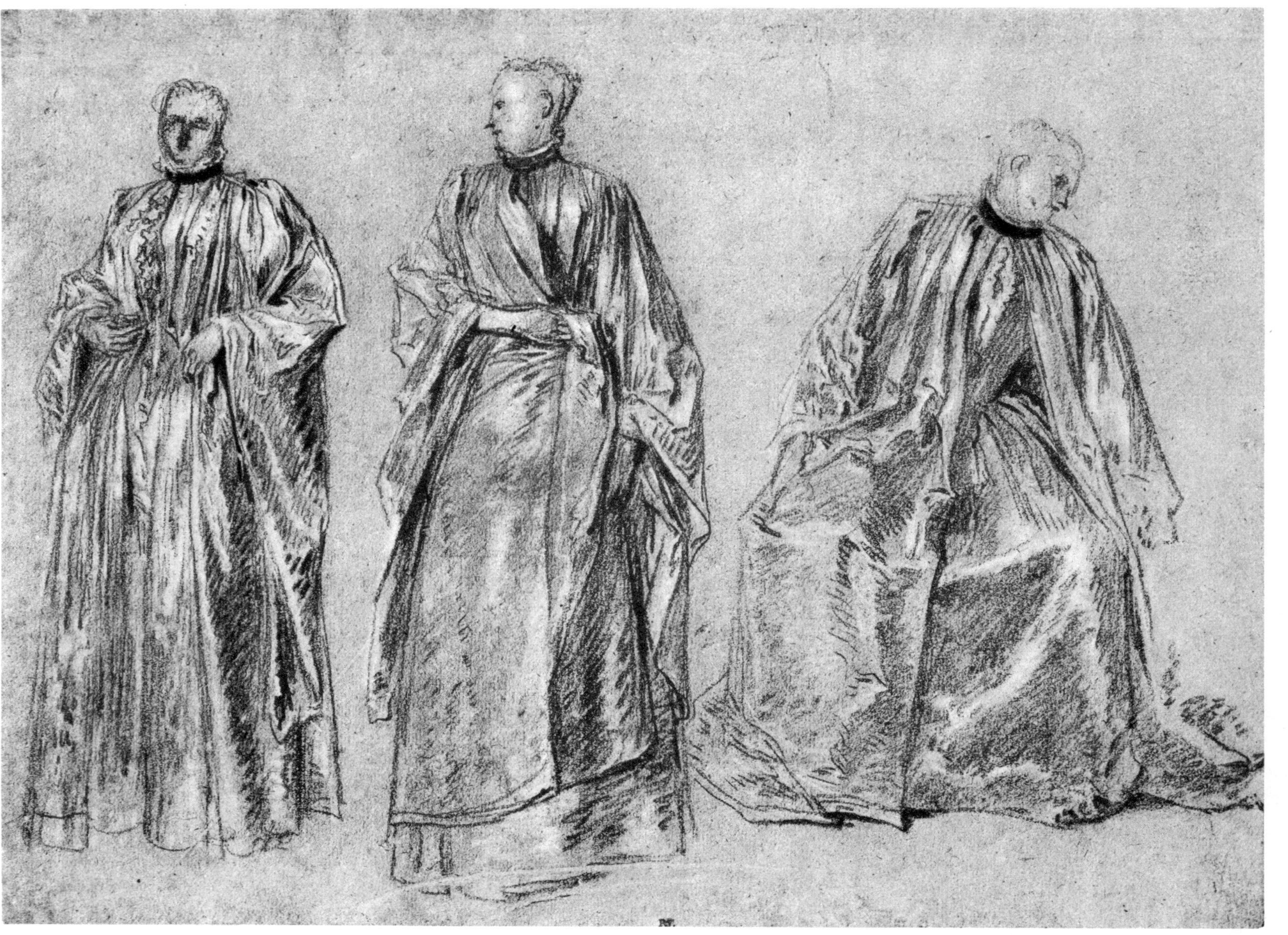

Three studies of a woman. Red, black and white chalk on gray paper; 253 × 342 mm.

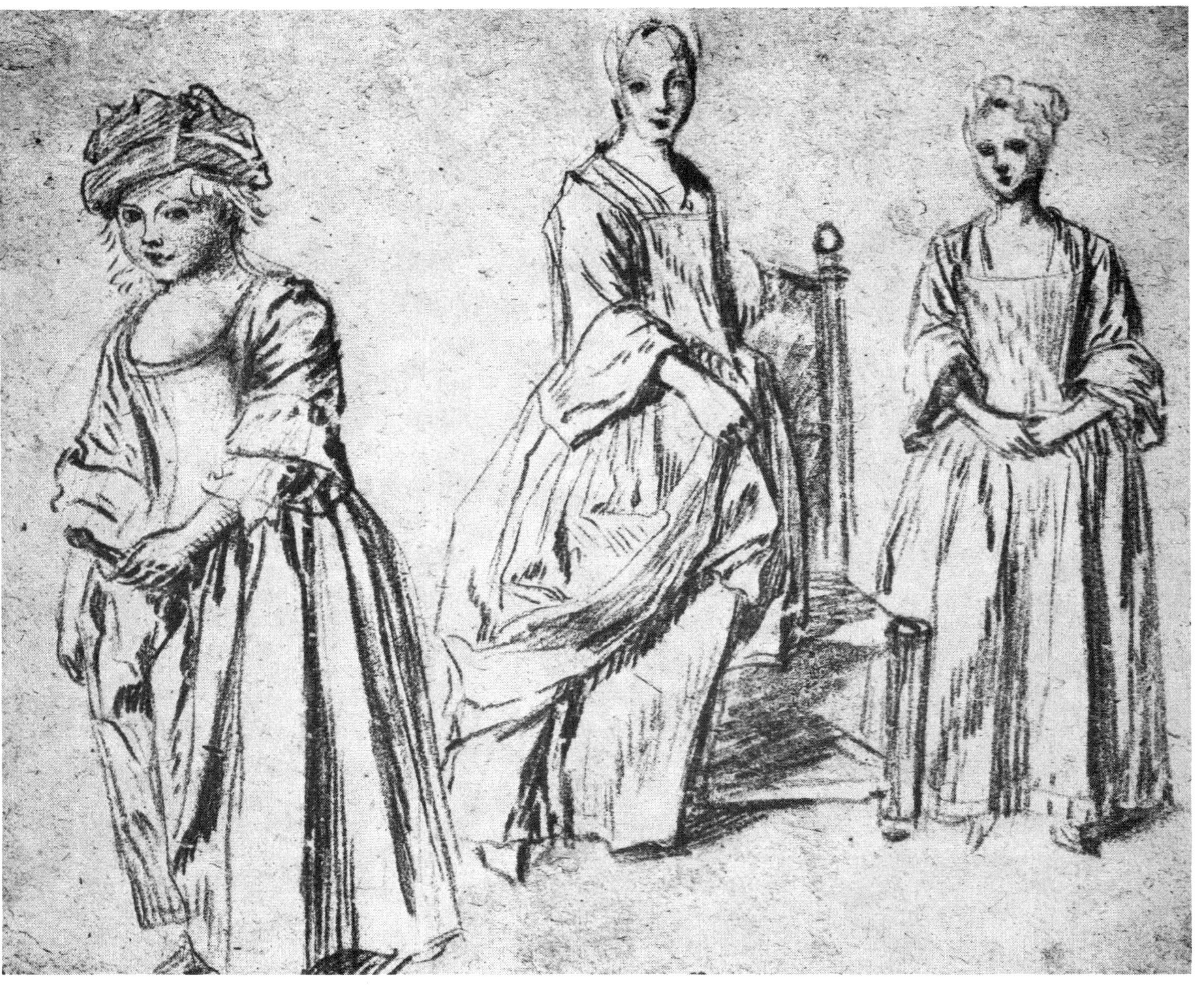

Girl standing; two girls, one of them resting one knee on a chair. Red chalk, white heightening, on gray paper; 253 × 298 mm.

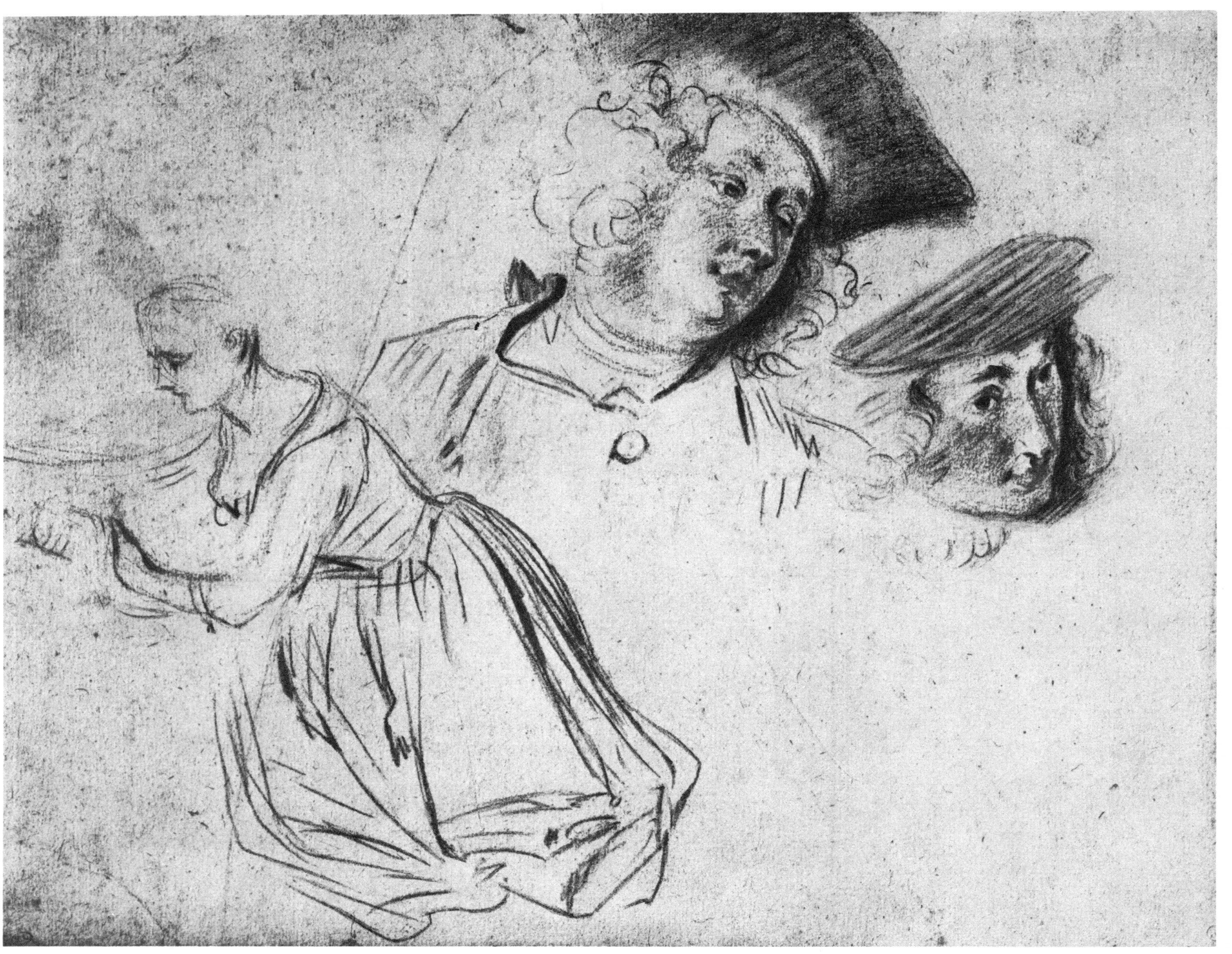

Two heads of young men wearing black hats; a young girl kneeling. Red, black and white chalk on gray paper; 263 × 334 mm.

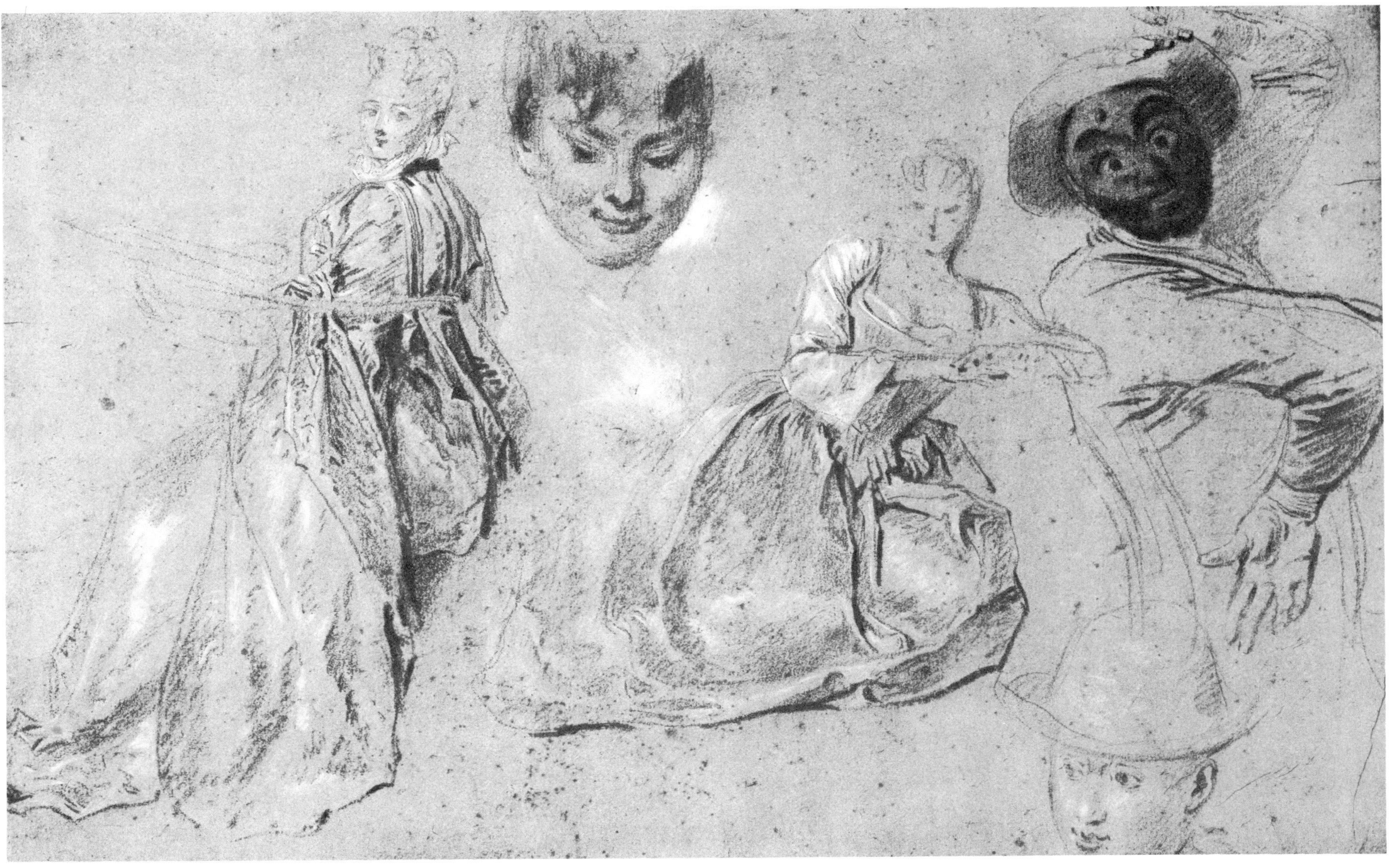

Two seated women; head of a woman; half-length portrait of Harlequin; head of Pierrot. Black, red and white chalk; 230 × 354 mm.

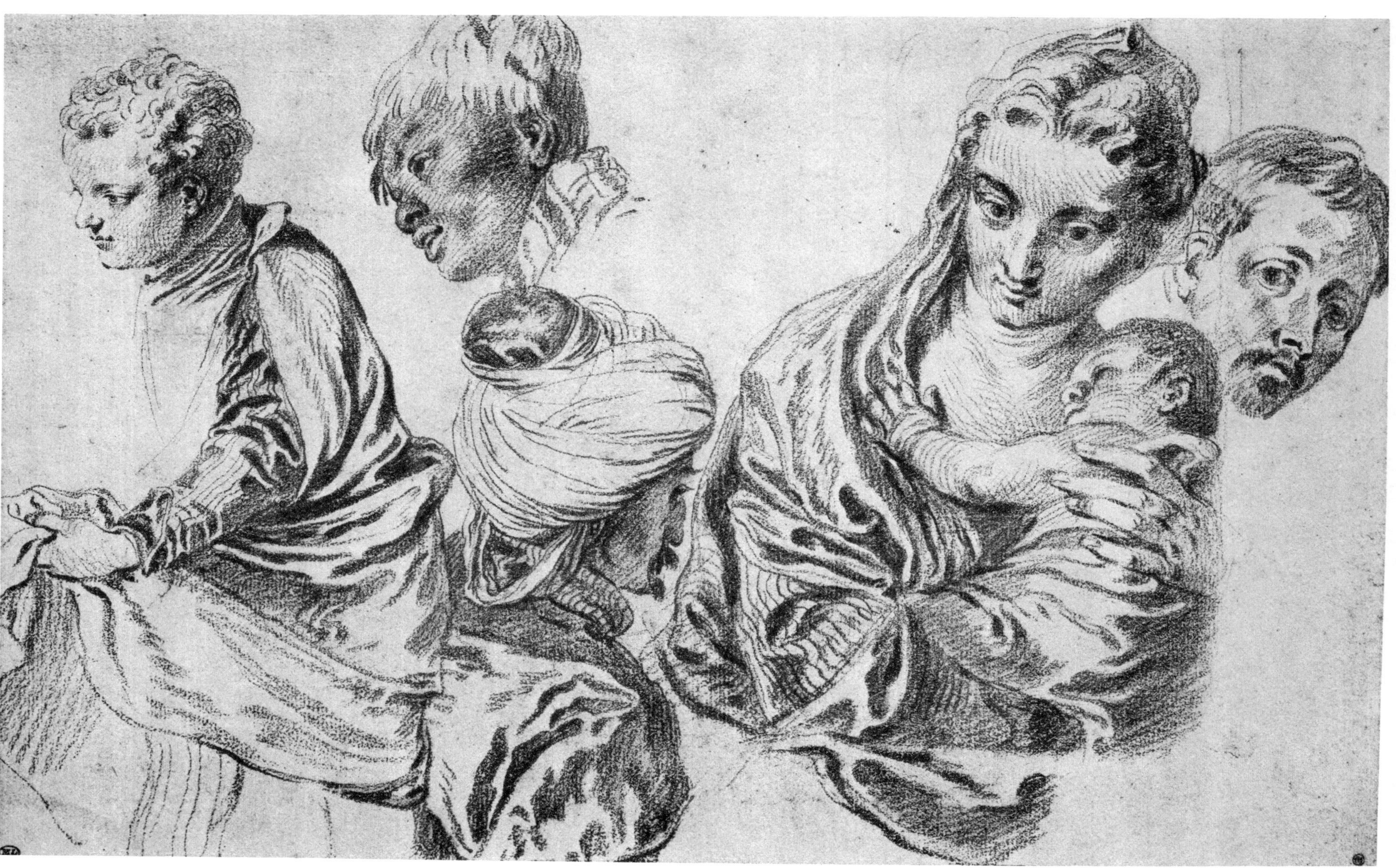

Studies after Veronese's *Adoration of the Magi*. Red chalk; 220 × 346 mm.

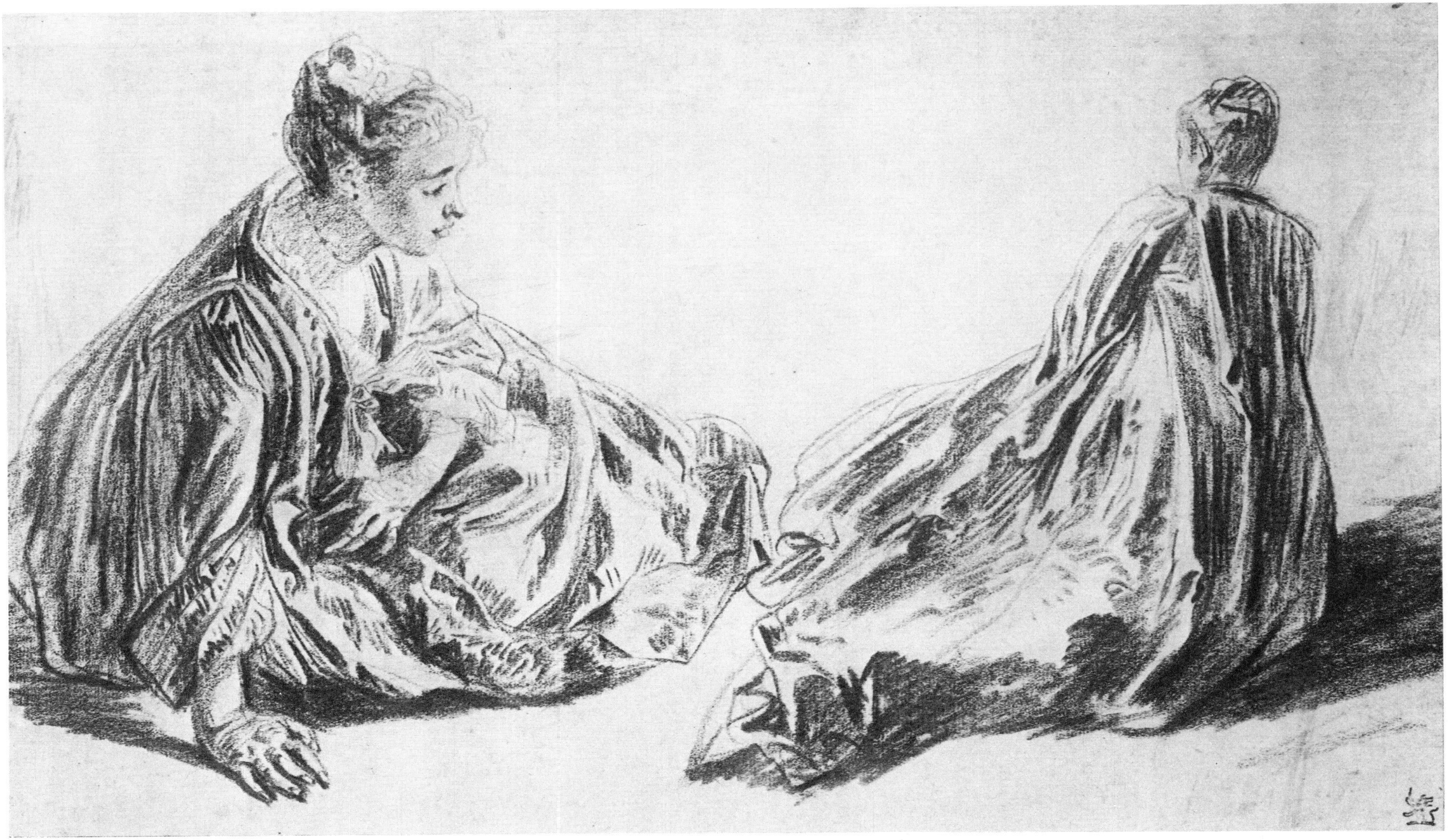

Two studies of a woman sitting on the ground. Red chalk; 200 × 340 mm.

Studies of three men. Red and white chalk on gray paper; 245 × 361 mm.

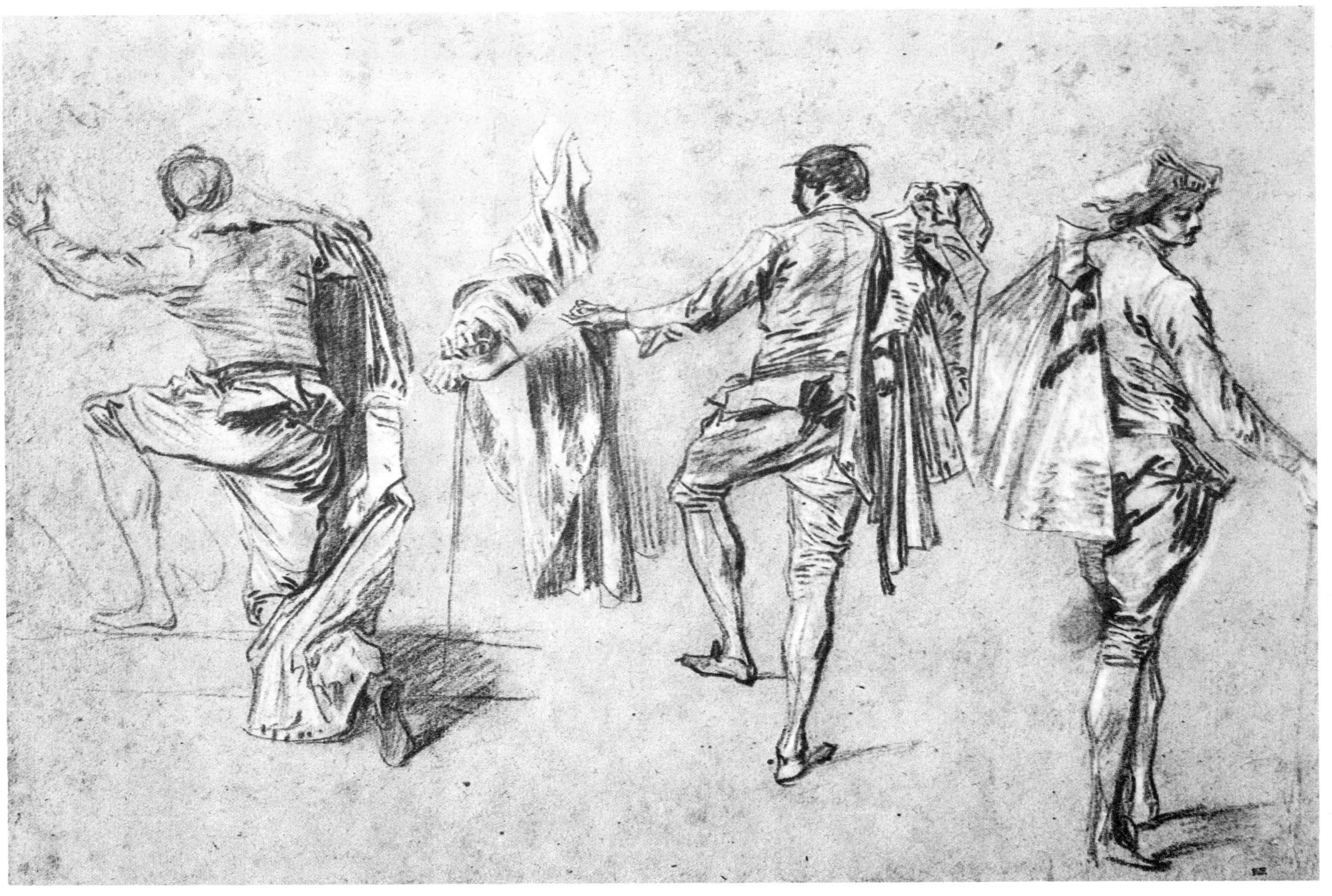

Three men; hands resting on a walking stick. Red and white chalk on gray paper; 269 × 312 mm.

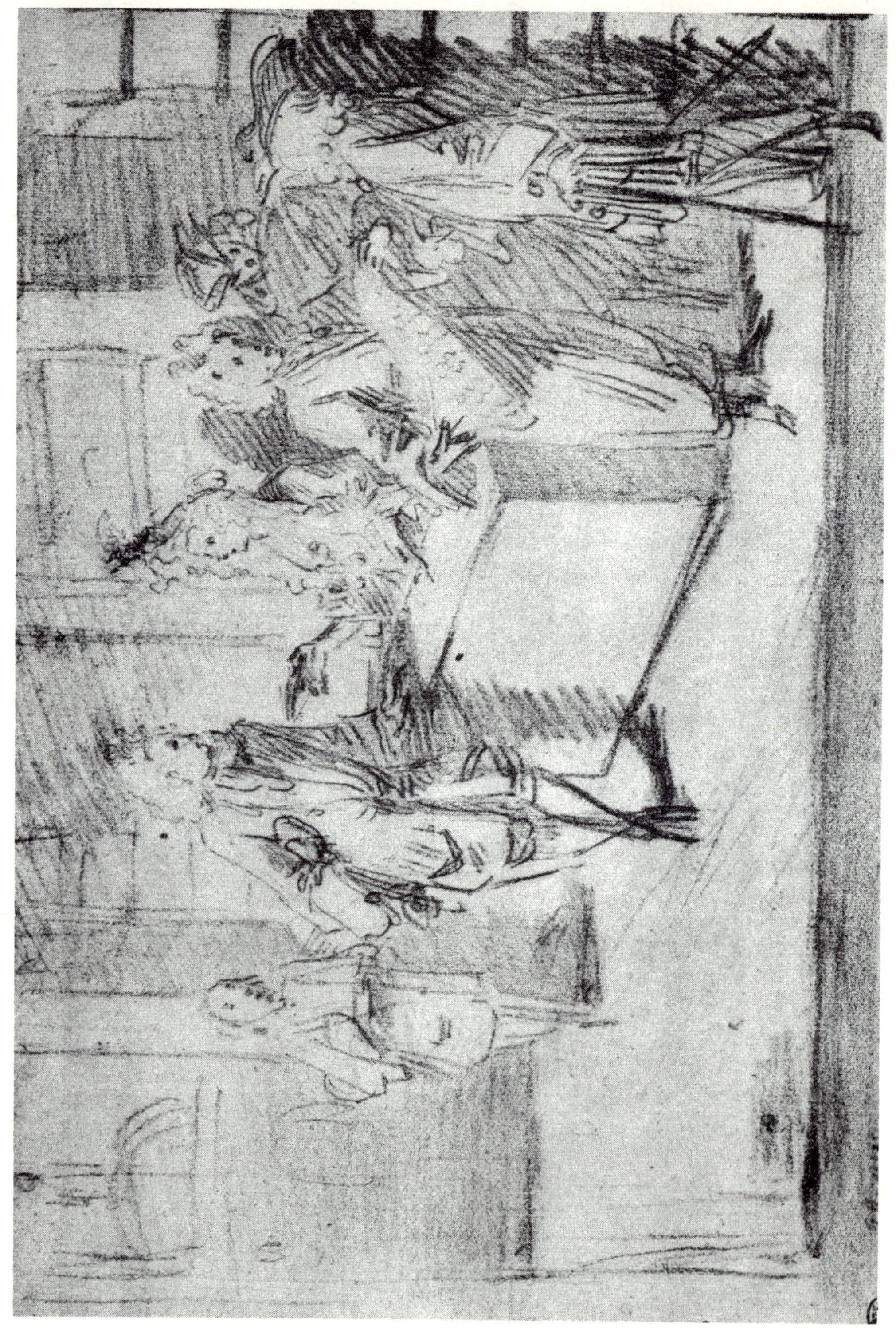

A draper's shop. Red chalk; 151 × 221 mm.

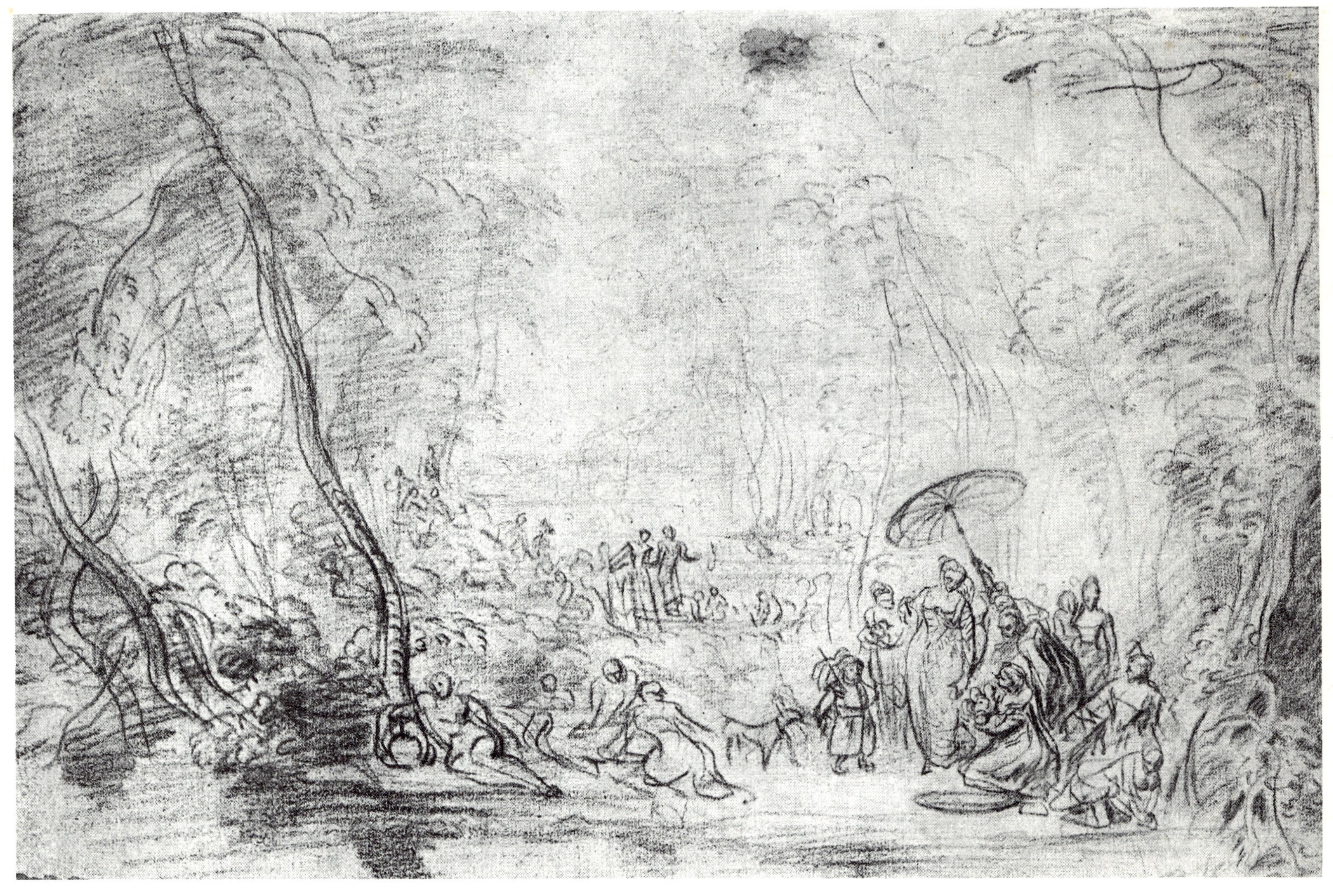

Moses rescued from the waters. Red chalk; 214 × 303 mm.

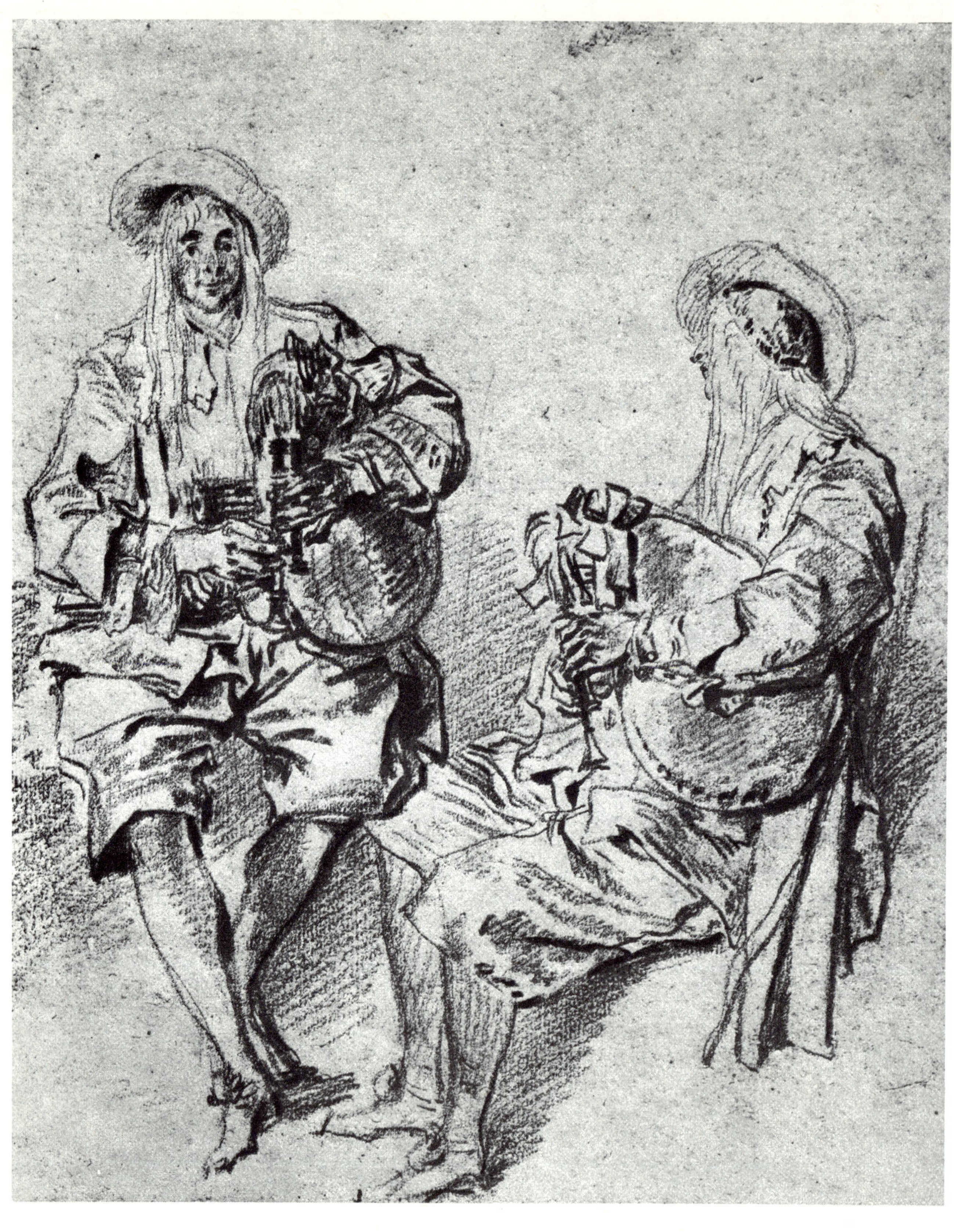

Two studies of a musette player. Red chalk, touches of black and white highlights, on gray paper; 271 × 222 mm.

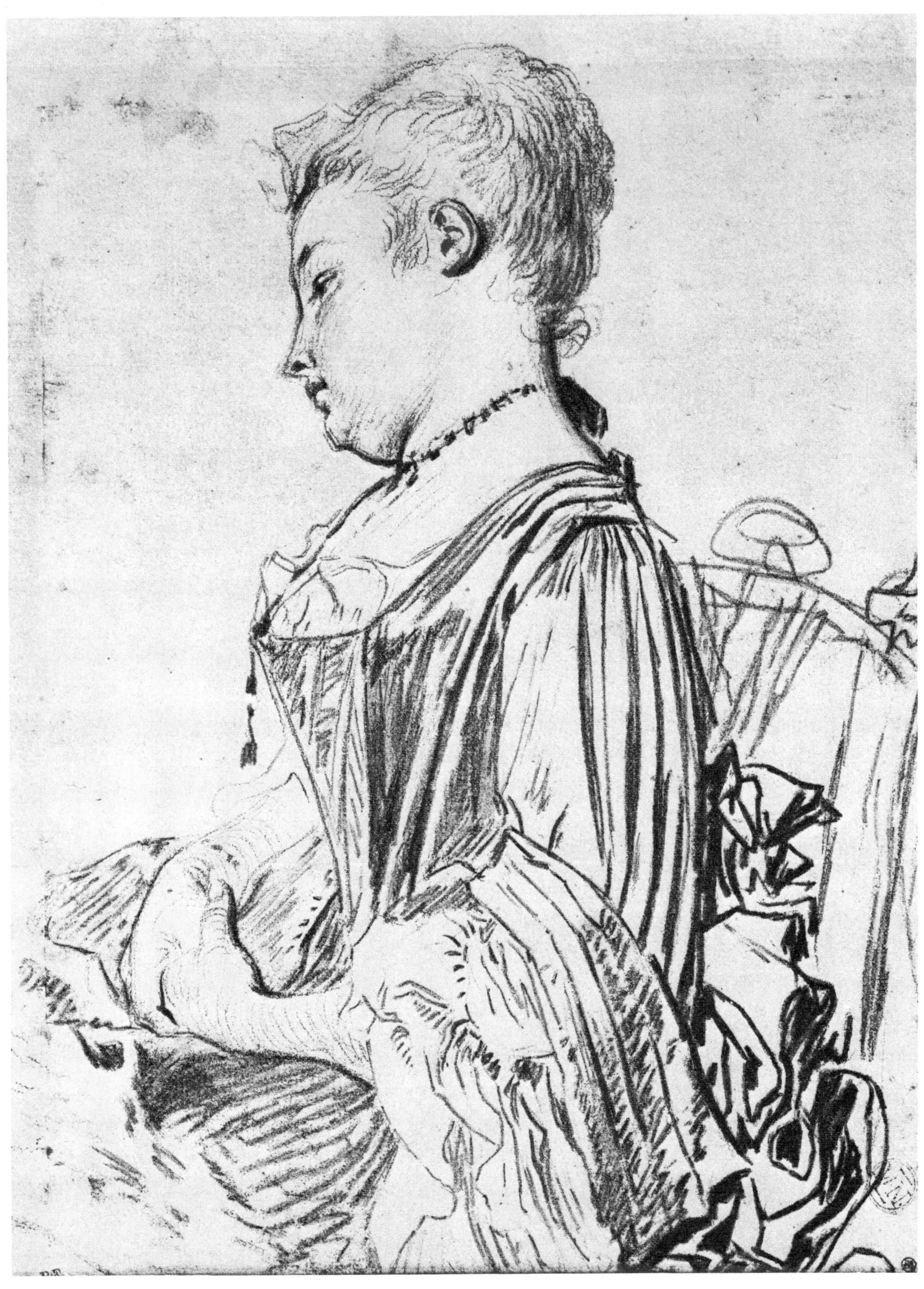

Young woman seated. Red and black chalk, some white highlights; 249 × 184 mm.

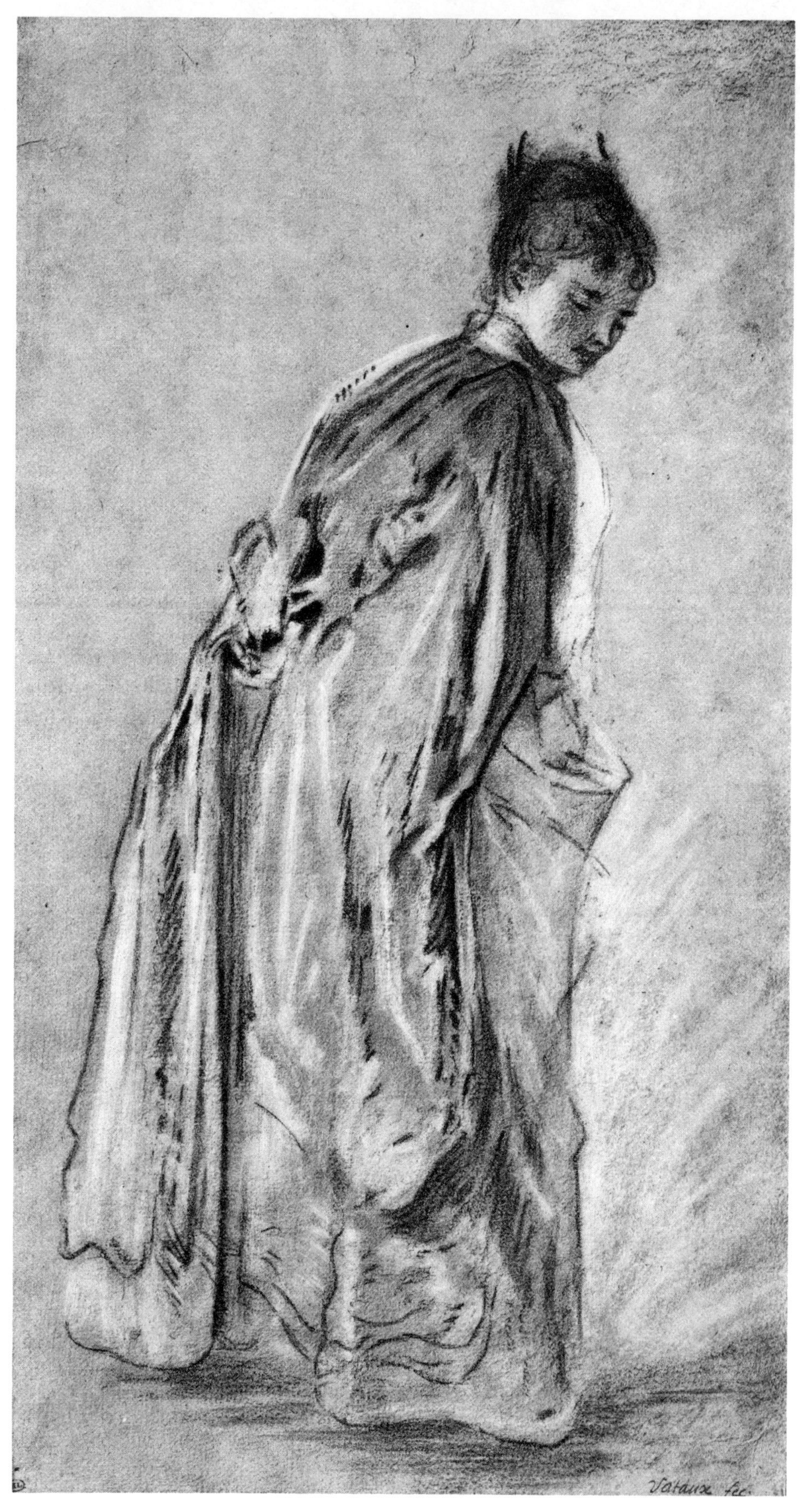

A woman. Black, red and white chalk on yellowish-gray paper; 424 × 228 mm.

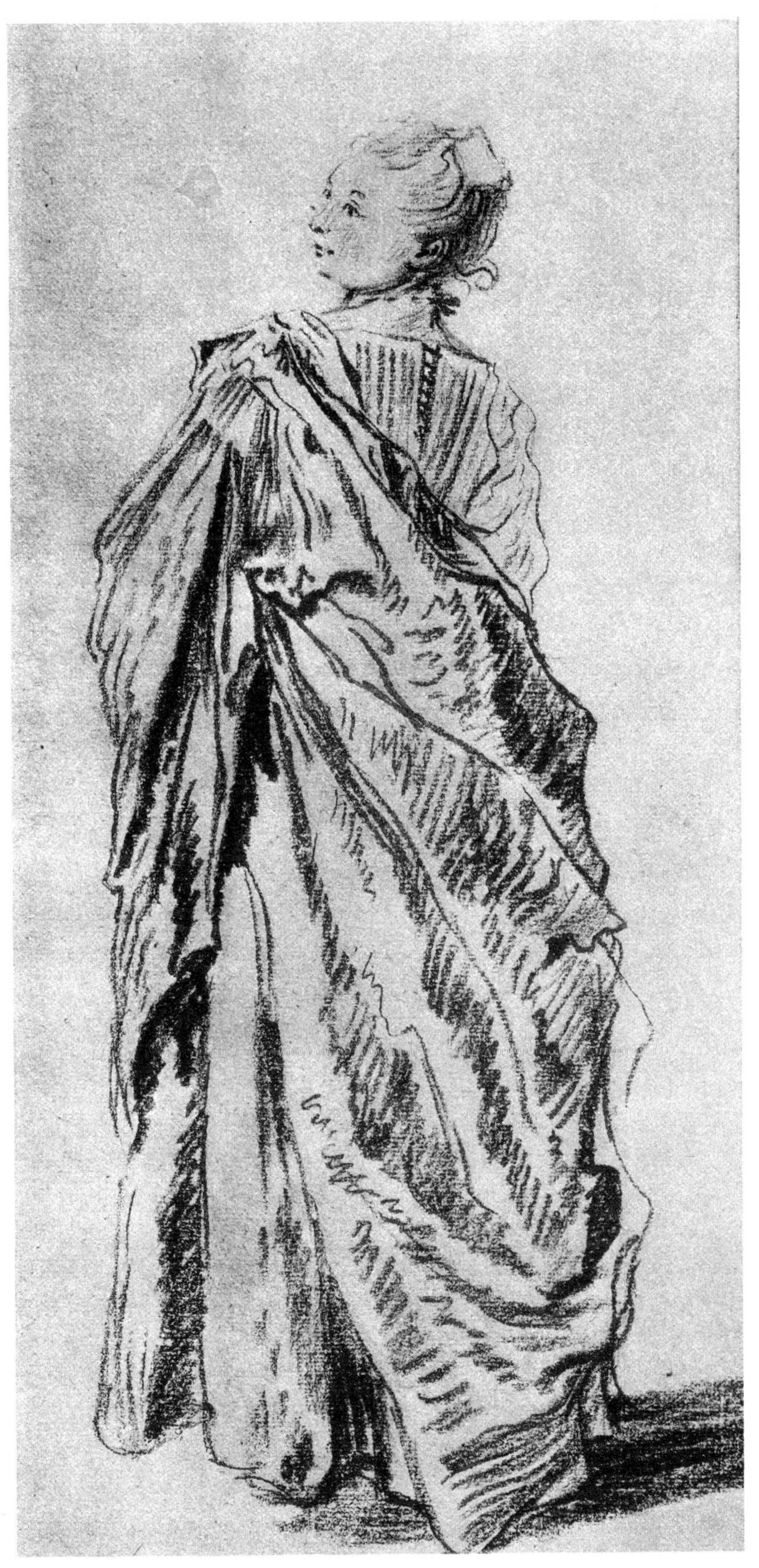

A woman. Black chalk, some red in the head; 334 × 165 mm.

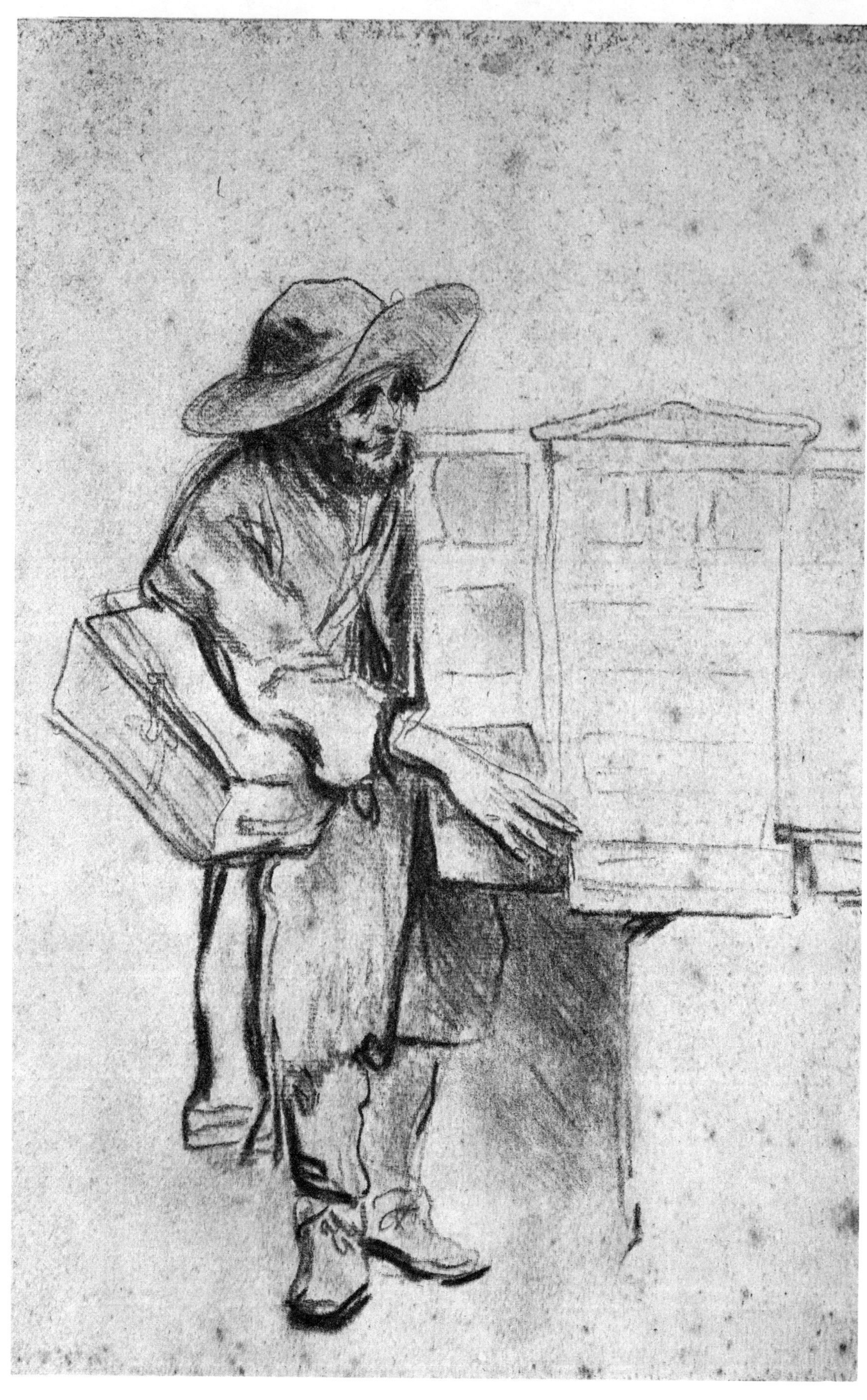

Itinerant showman from Savoy with a raree show. Red and black chalk; 315 × 210 mm.

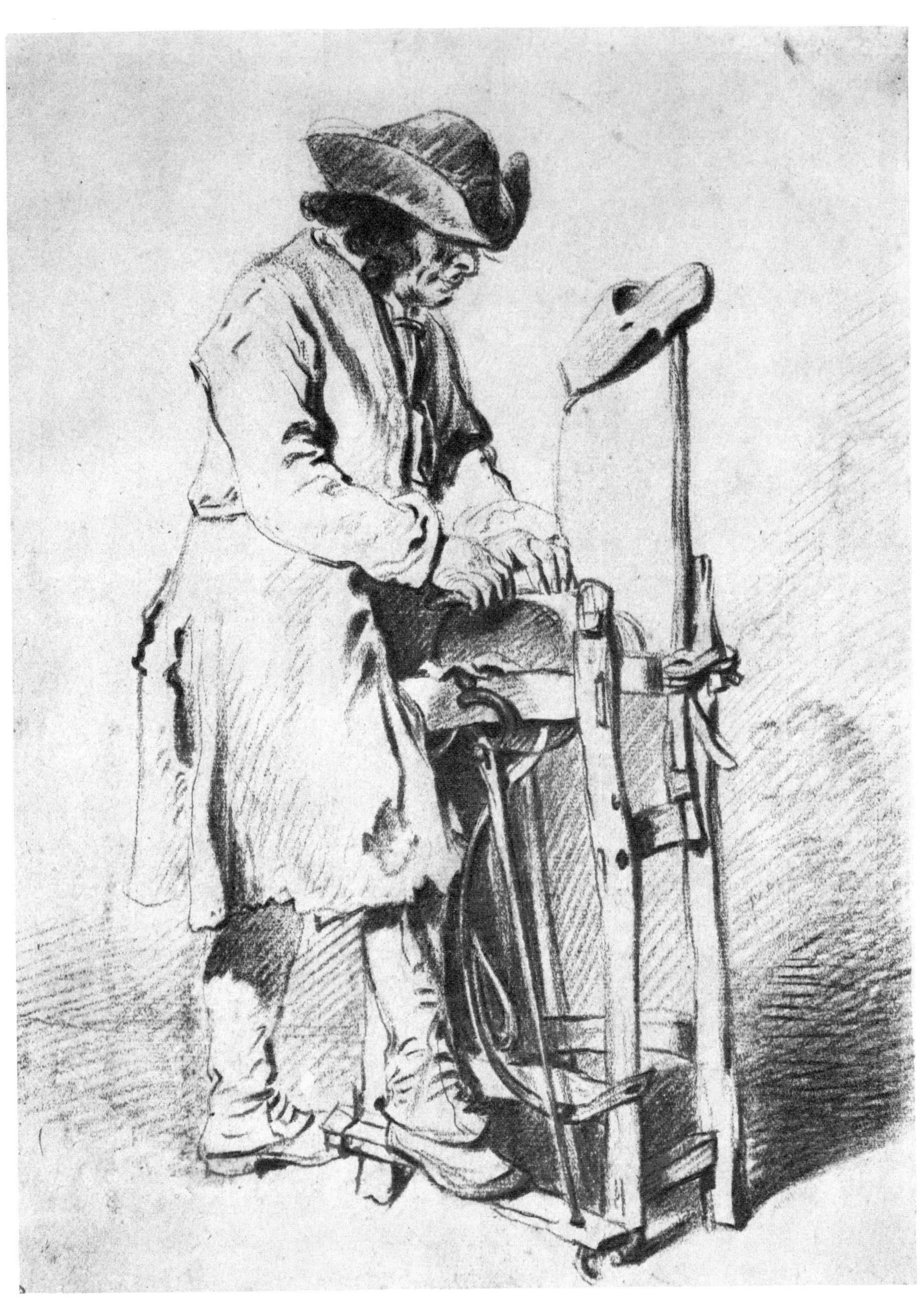

A knife grinder. Red chalk, black heightening, on cream-colored paper; 289 × 215 mm.

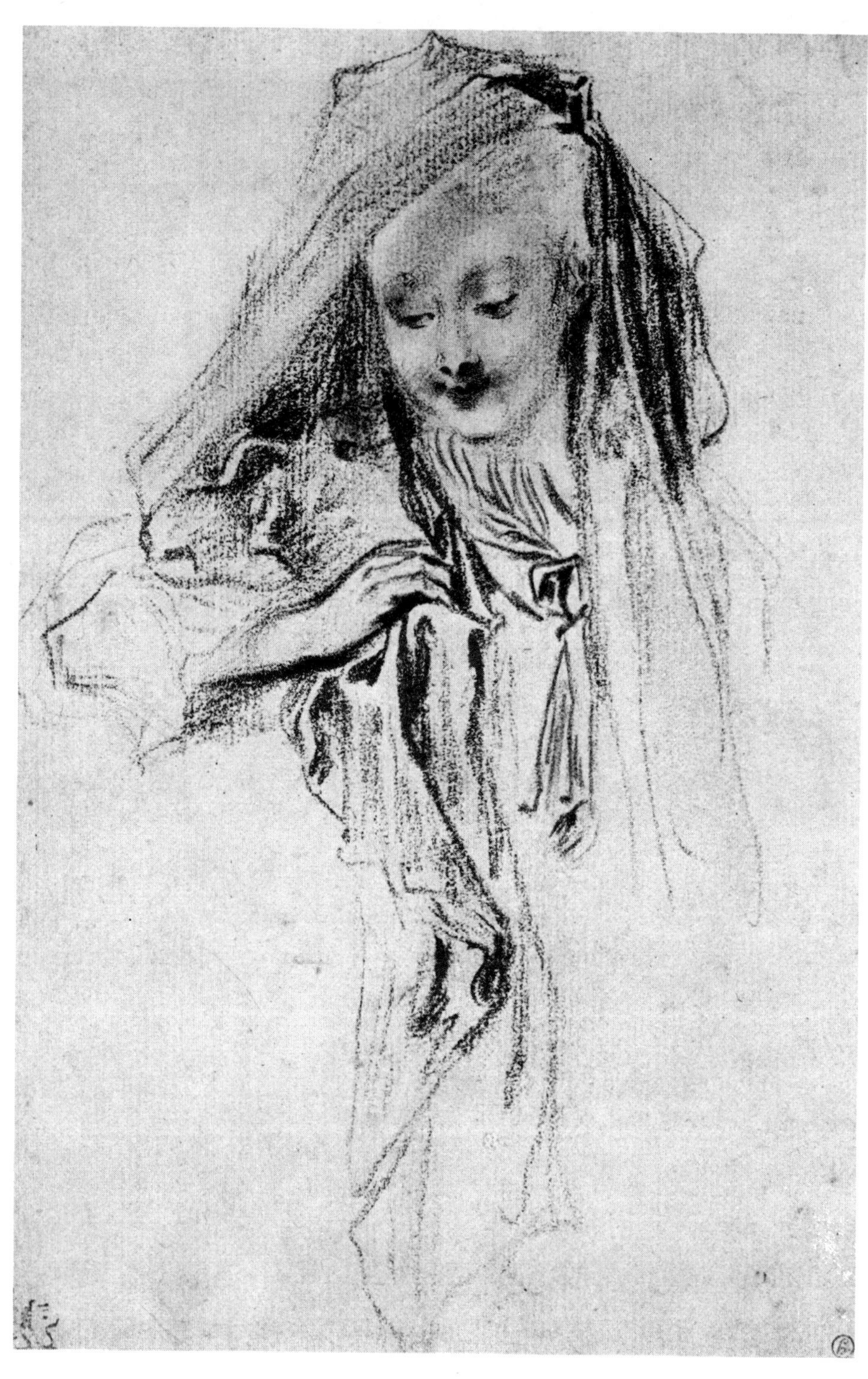

A woman. Black and red chalk; 180 × 120 mm.

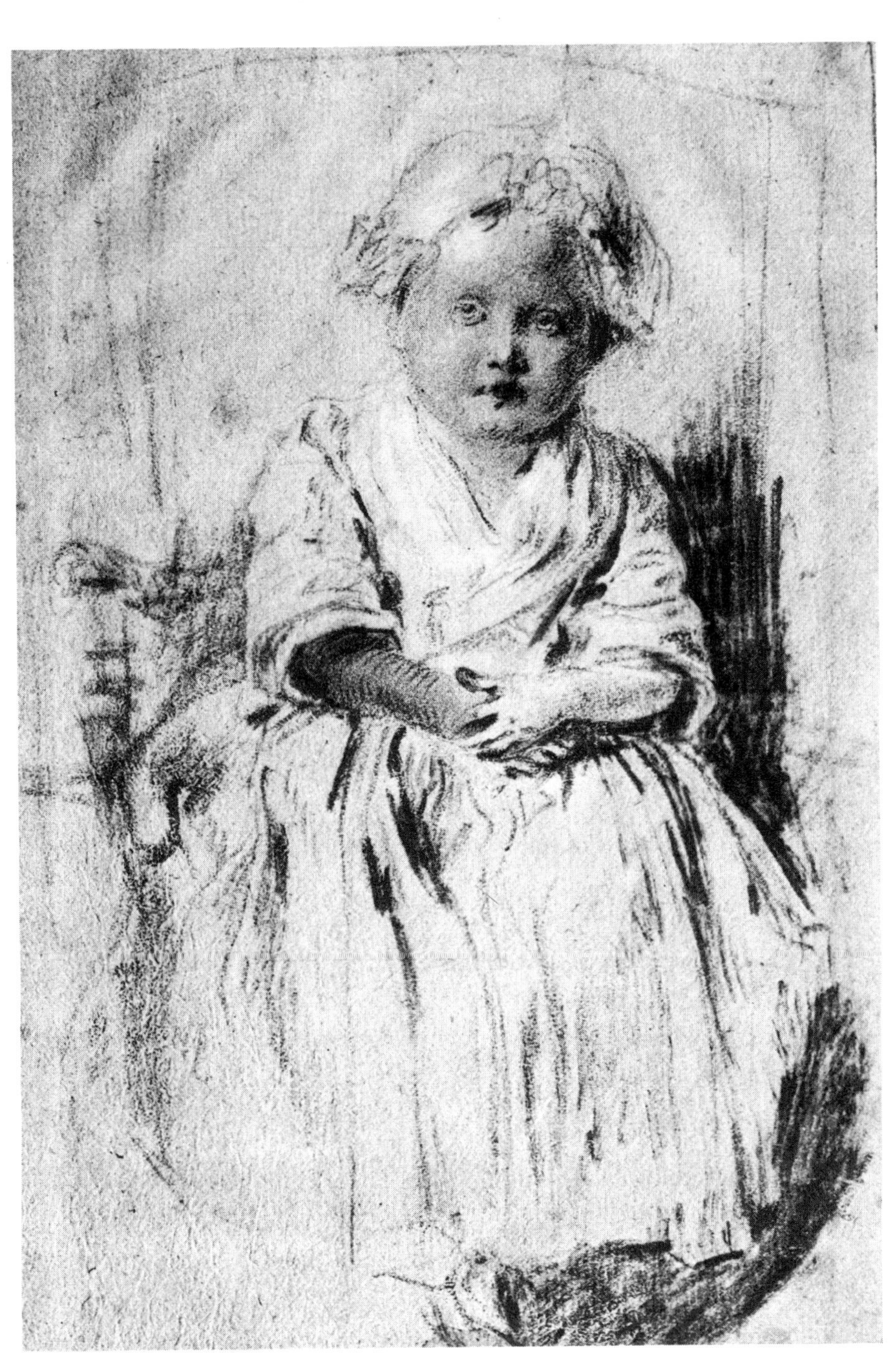

Little girl, seated. Black, red and white chalk; 170 × 120 mm.

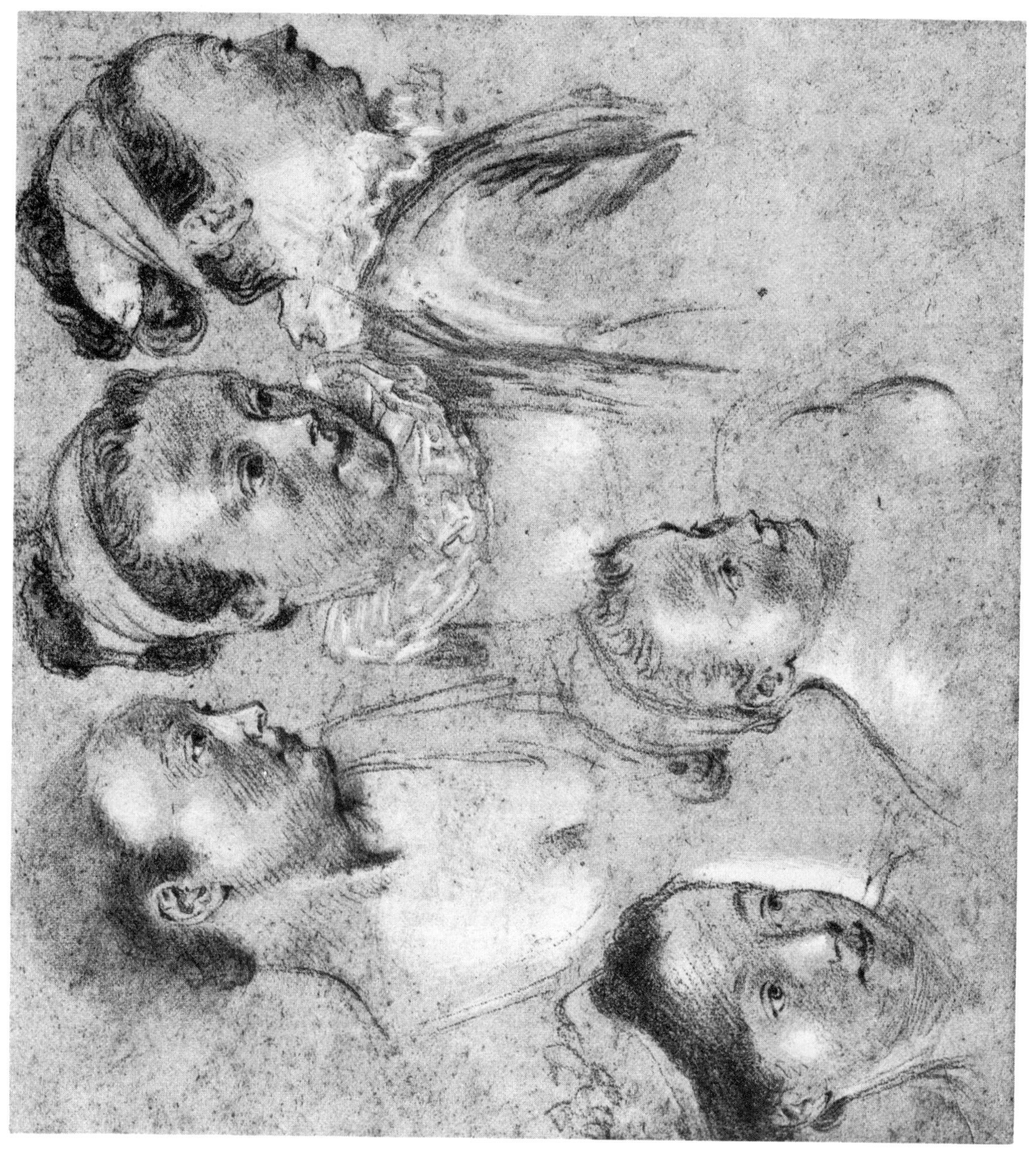

Five heads of young women. Red, black and white chalk on gray paper; 217 × 229 mm.

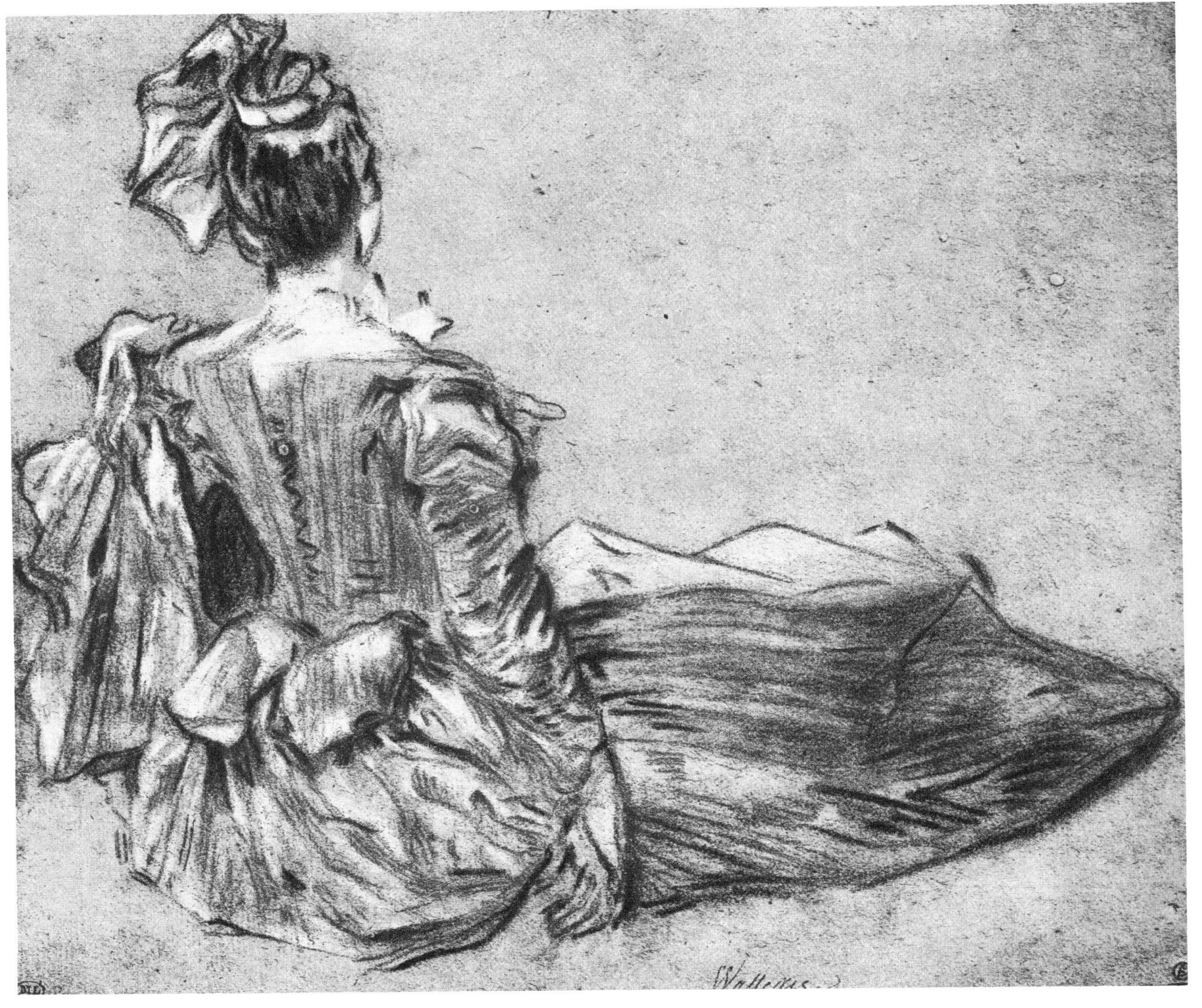

Woman sitting on the ground. Red, black and white chalk on gray paper; 191 × 220 mm.

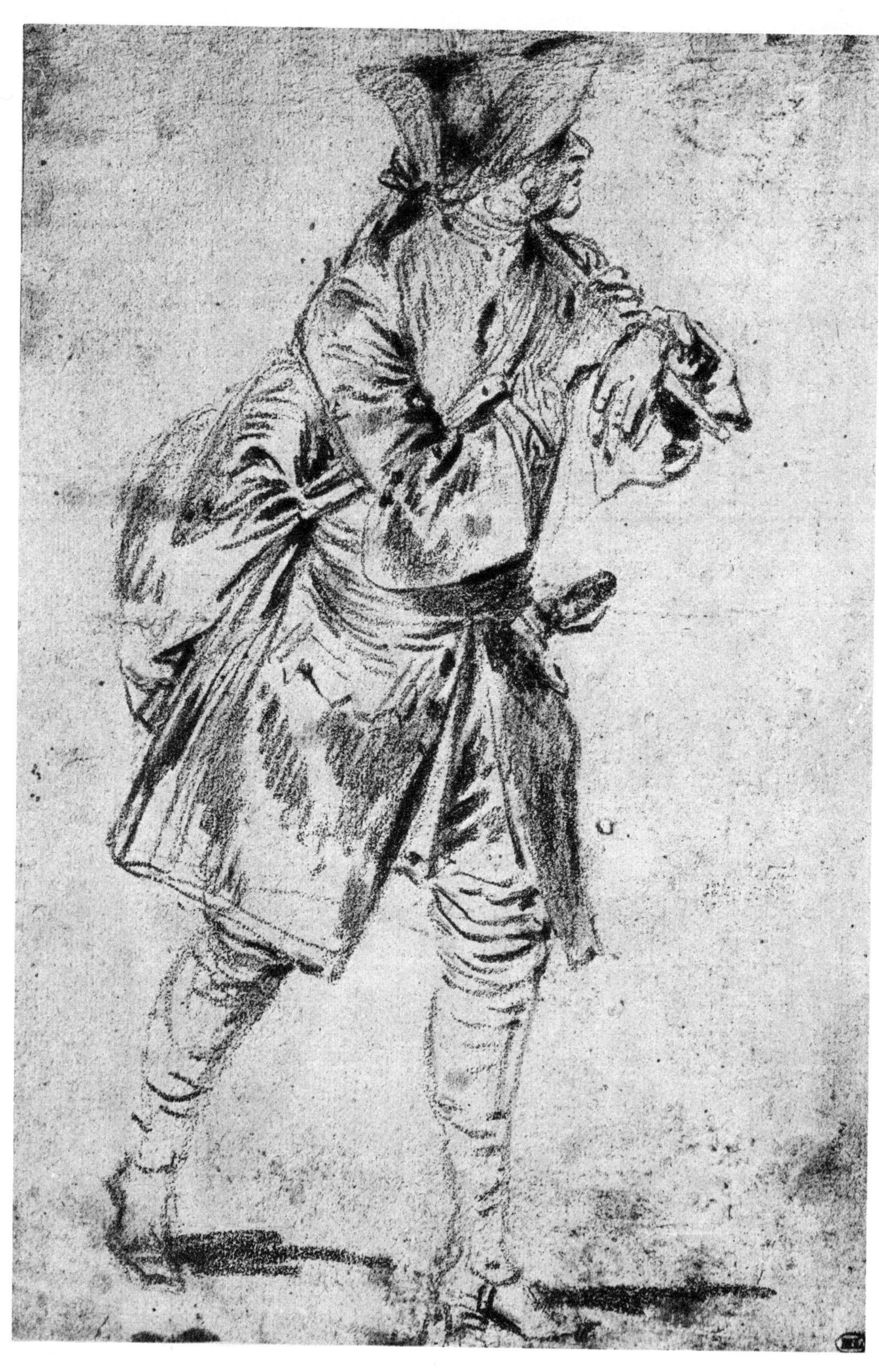

Soldier on the march. Red chalk; 217 × 140 mm.

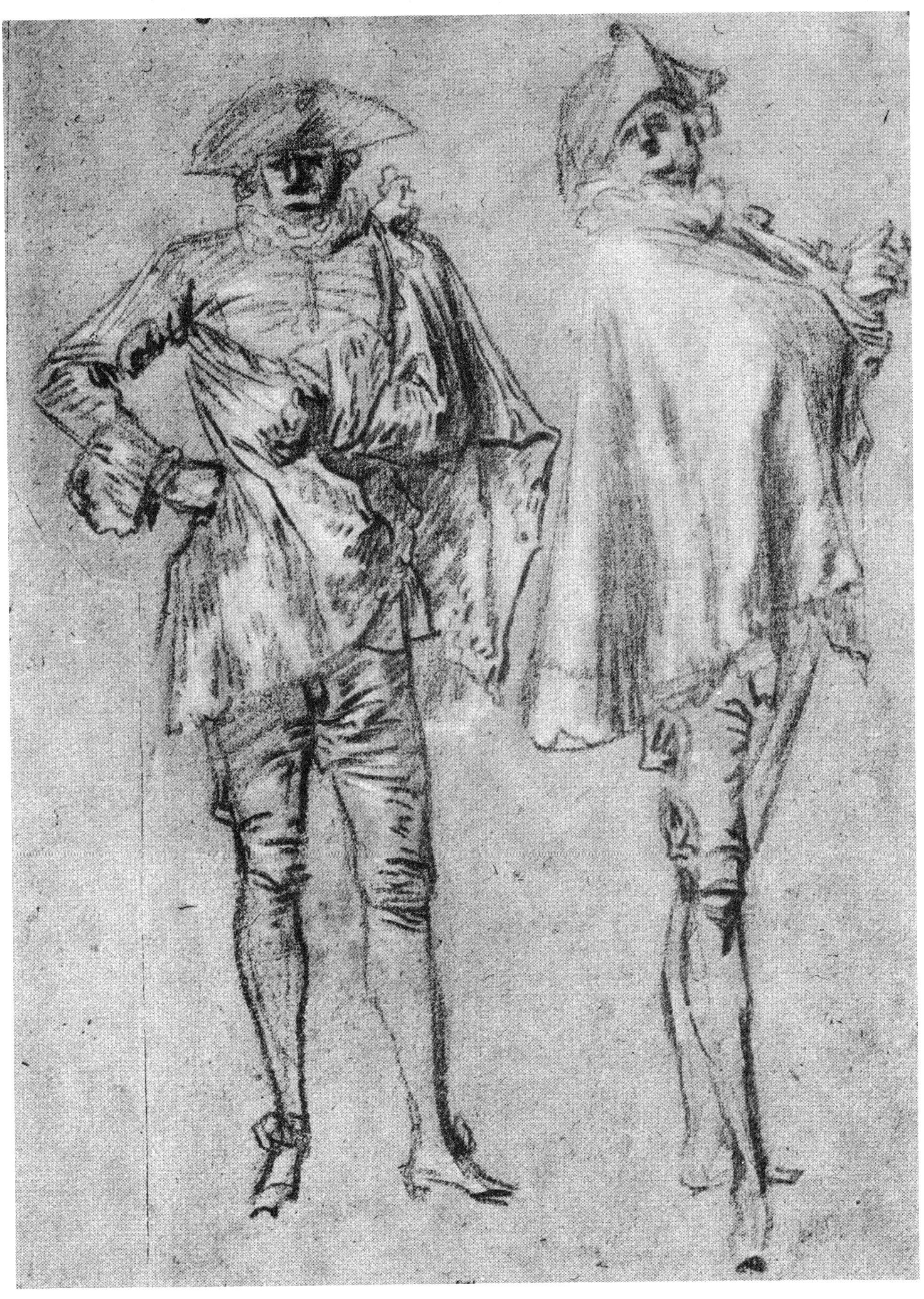

Two studies of a man. Red and white chalk on gray paper; 247 × 182 mm.

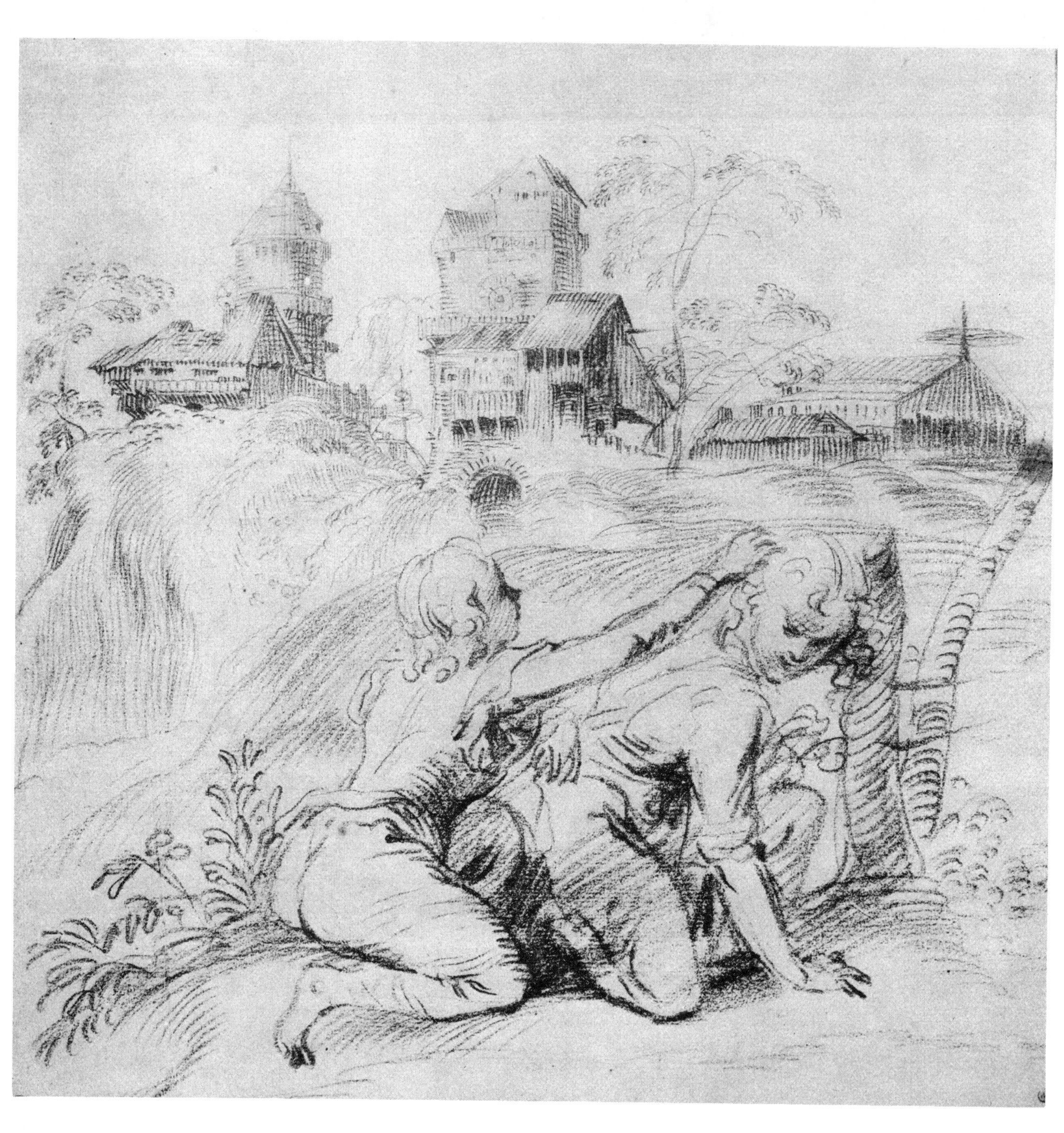

Landscape with two figures in the foreground, after Titian. Red chalk; 234 × 233 mm.

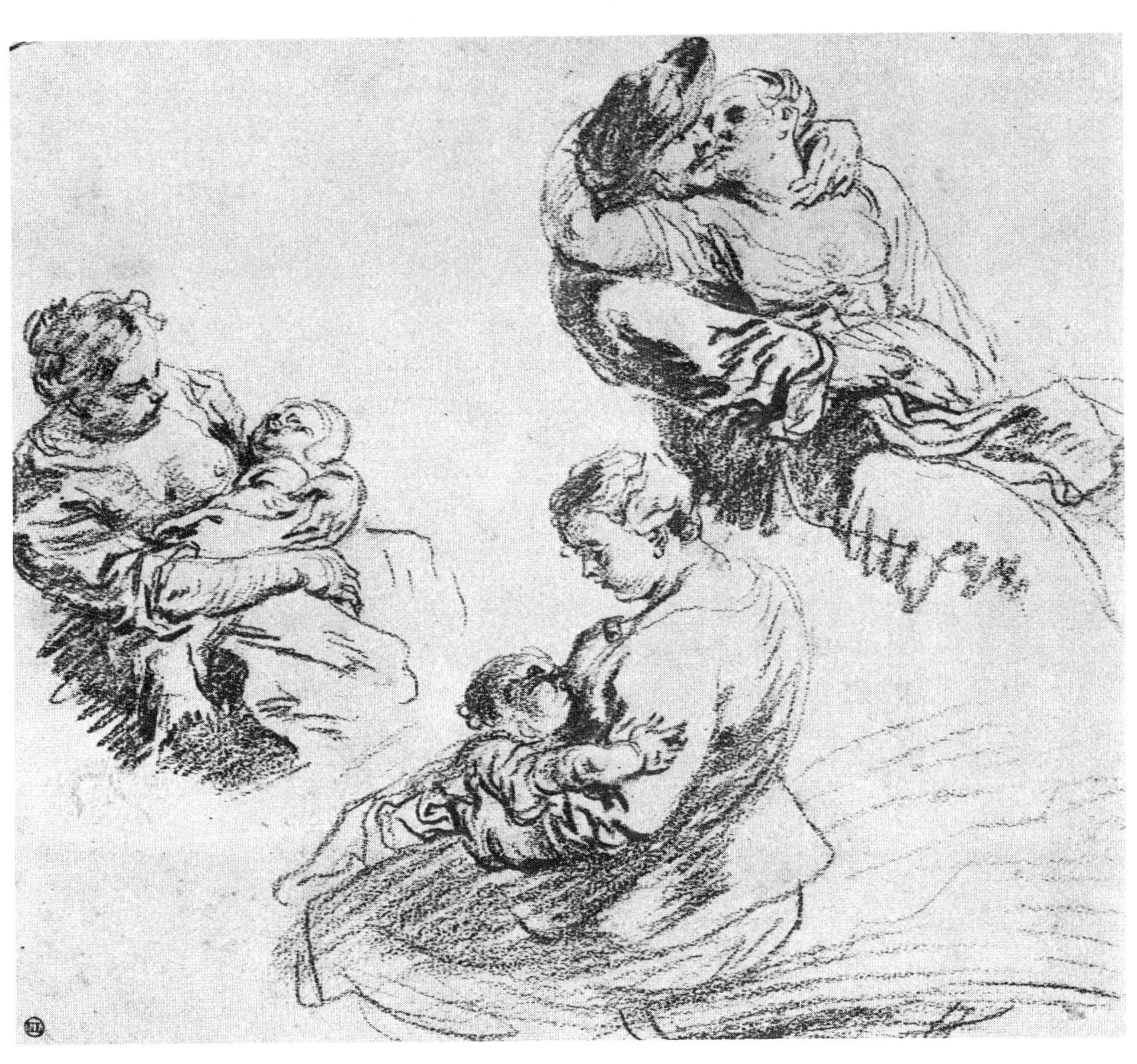

Study after Rubens' *Kermesse*. Red chalk; 170 × 200 mm.

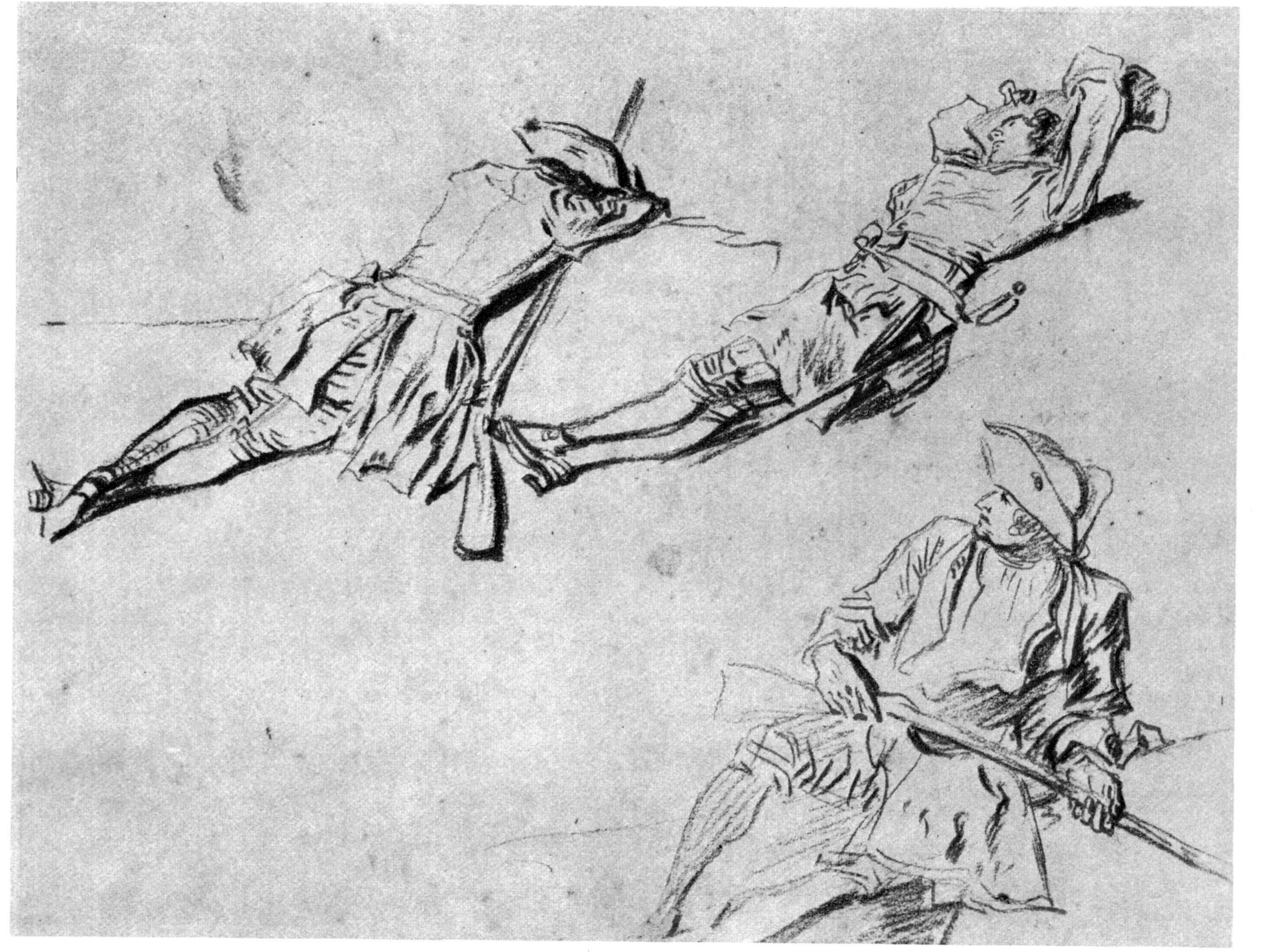

Three soldiers resting. Red chalk; 174 × 218 mm.

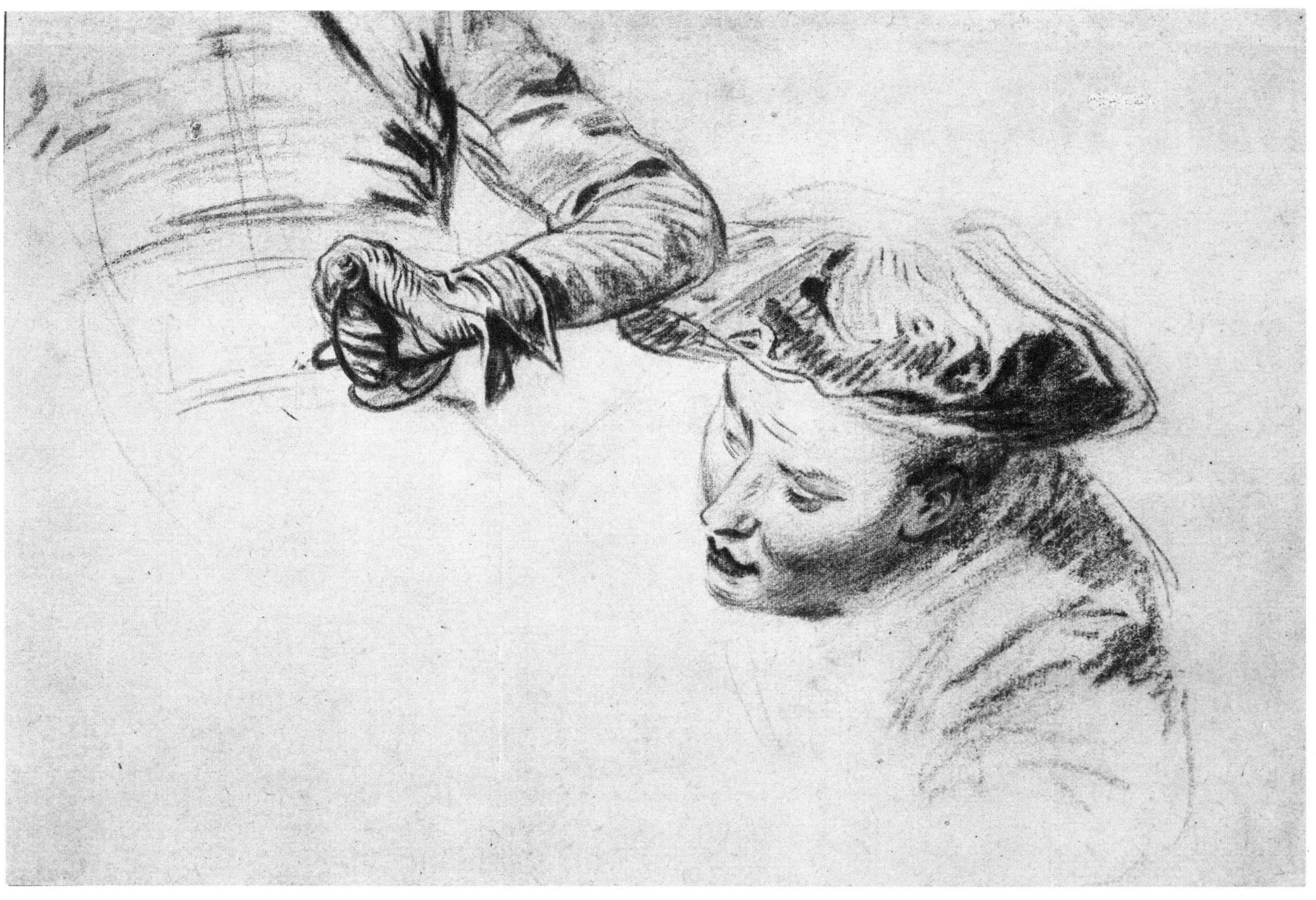

The arm of Crispin, the hand on the hilt of a sword; the head of a man wearing a beret. Black chalk, red heightening; 179 × 255 mm.

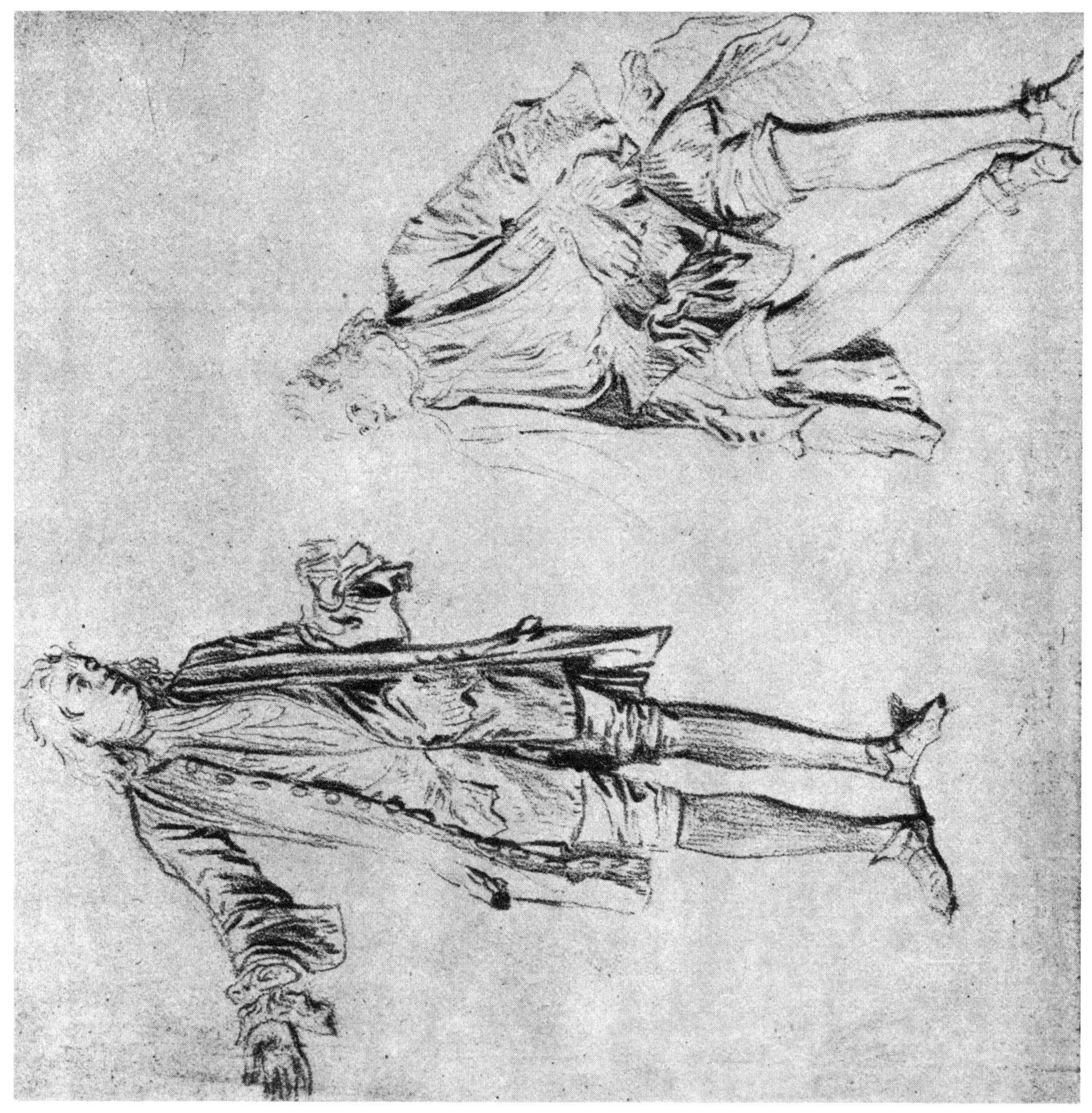

Two men. Red chalk; 181 × 176 mm. (the sheet extended 15 mm. to the left; the left hand of the standing figure is redone).

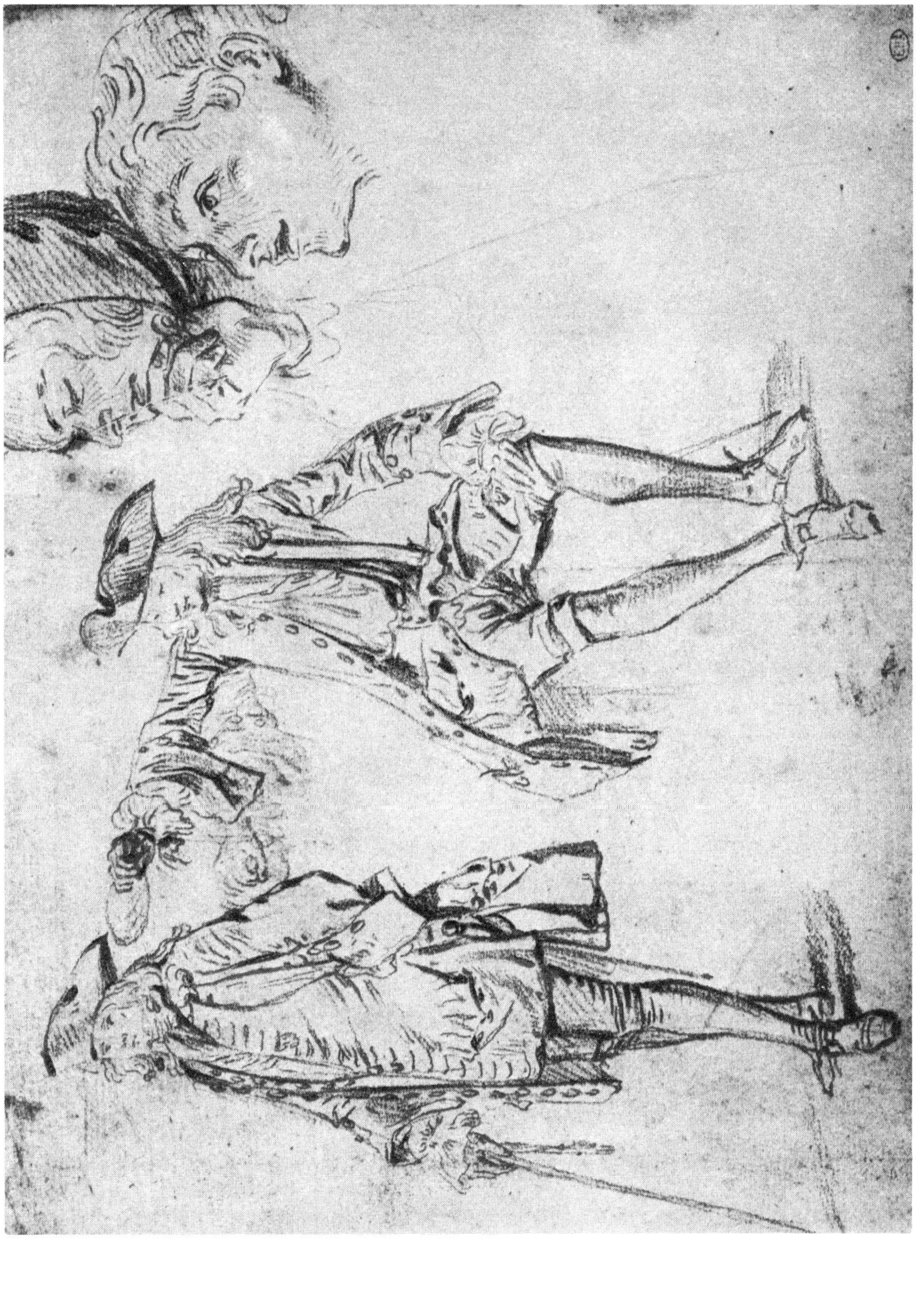

Two men; the heads of two women. Red chalk; 160 × 204 mm.

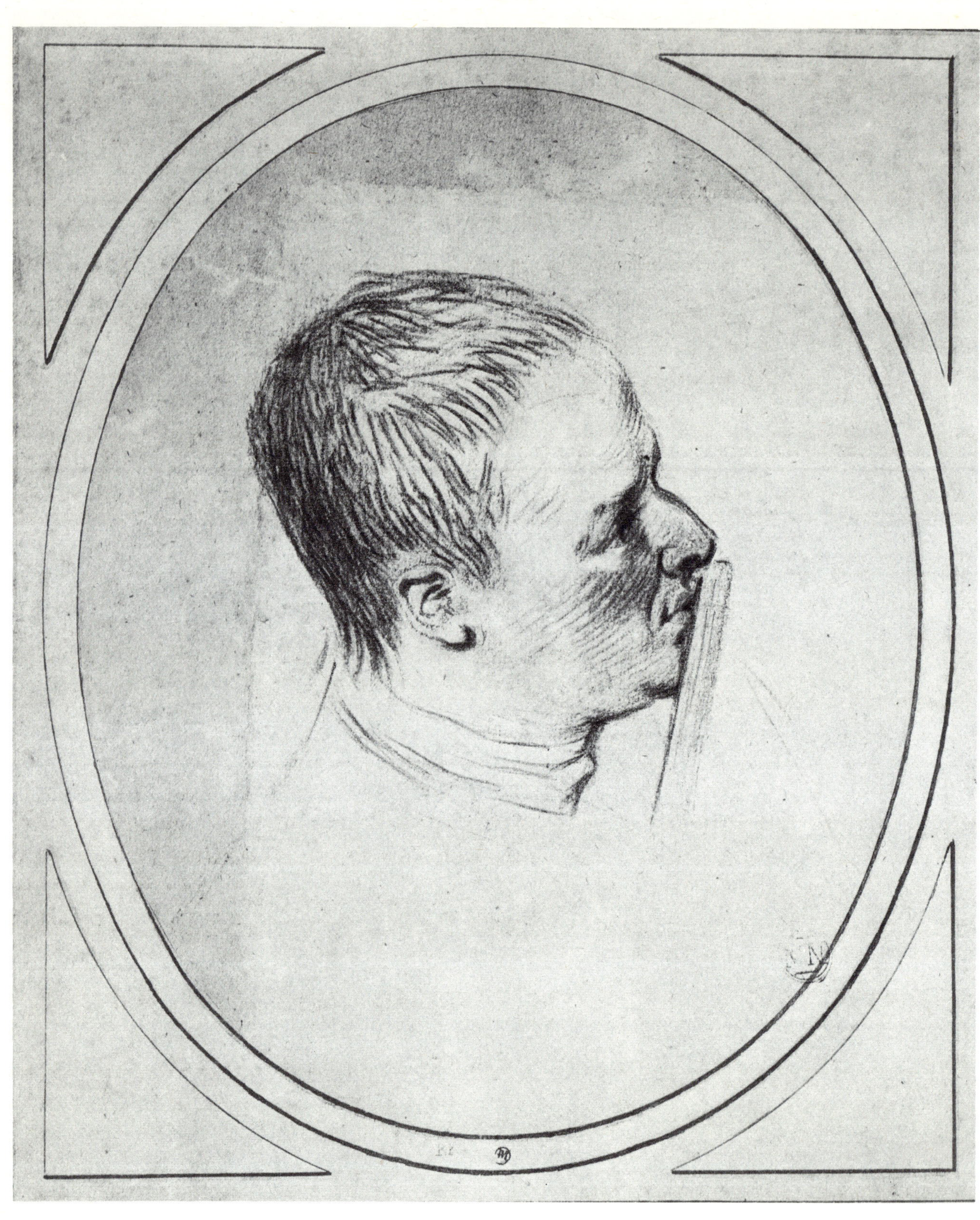

Head of a man playing the flute. Red and black chalk, some white highlights; 187 × 155 mm.

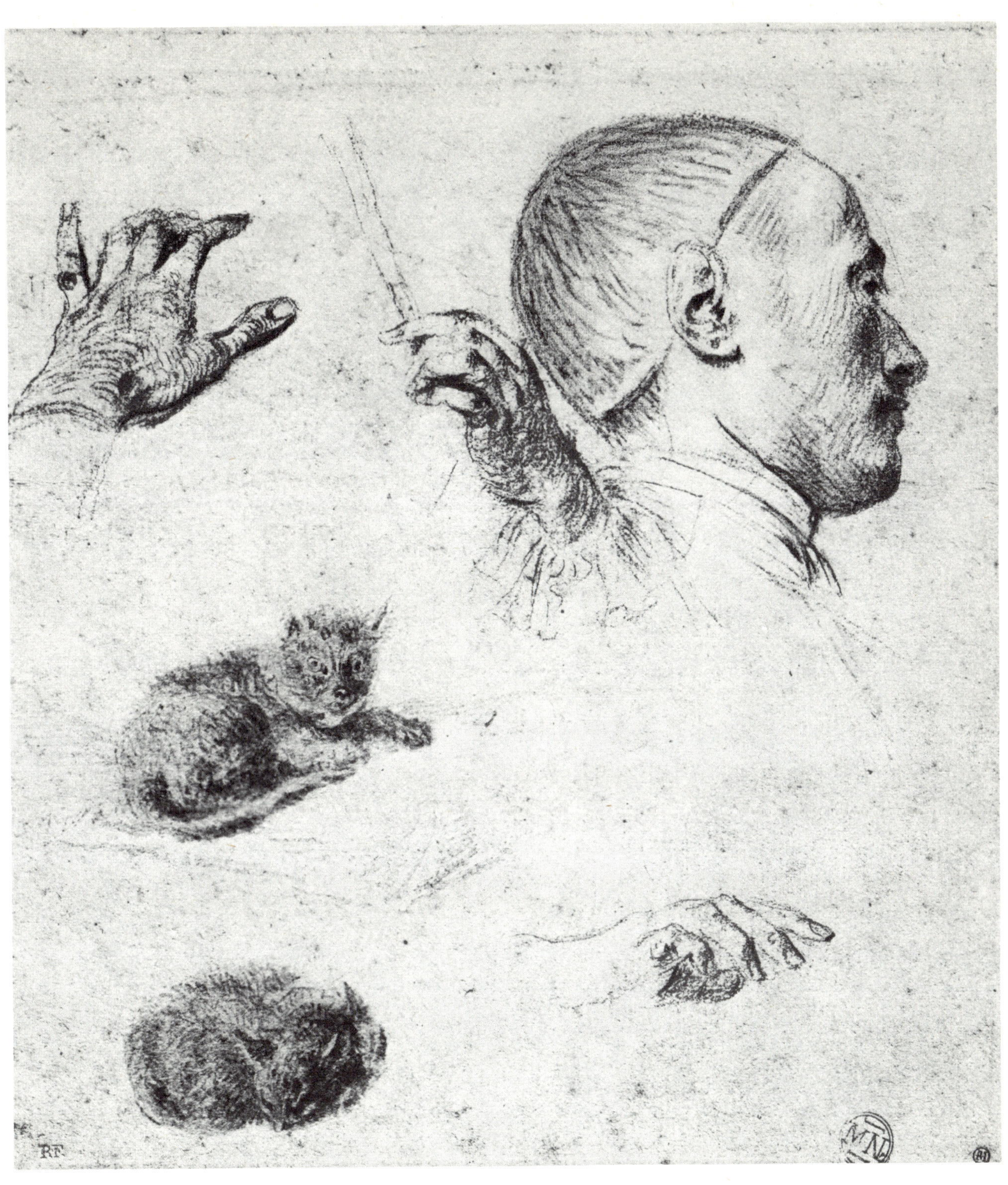

Head of a man; three hands; two studies of a cat. Red chalk, black lead, some touches of wash; 200 × 180 mm.

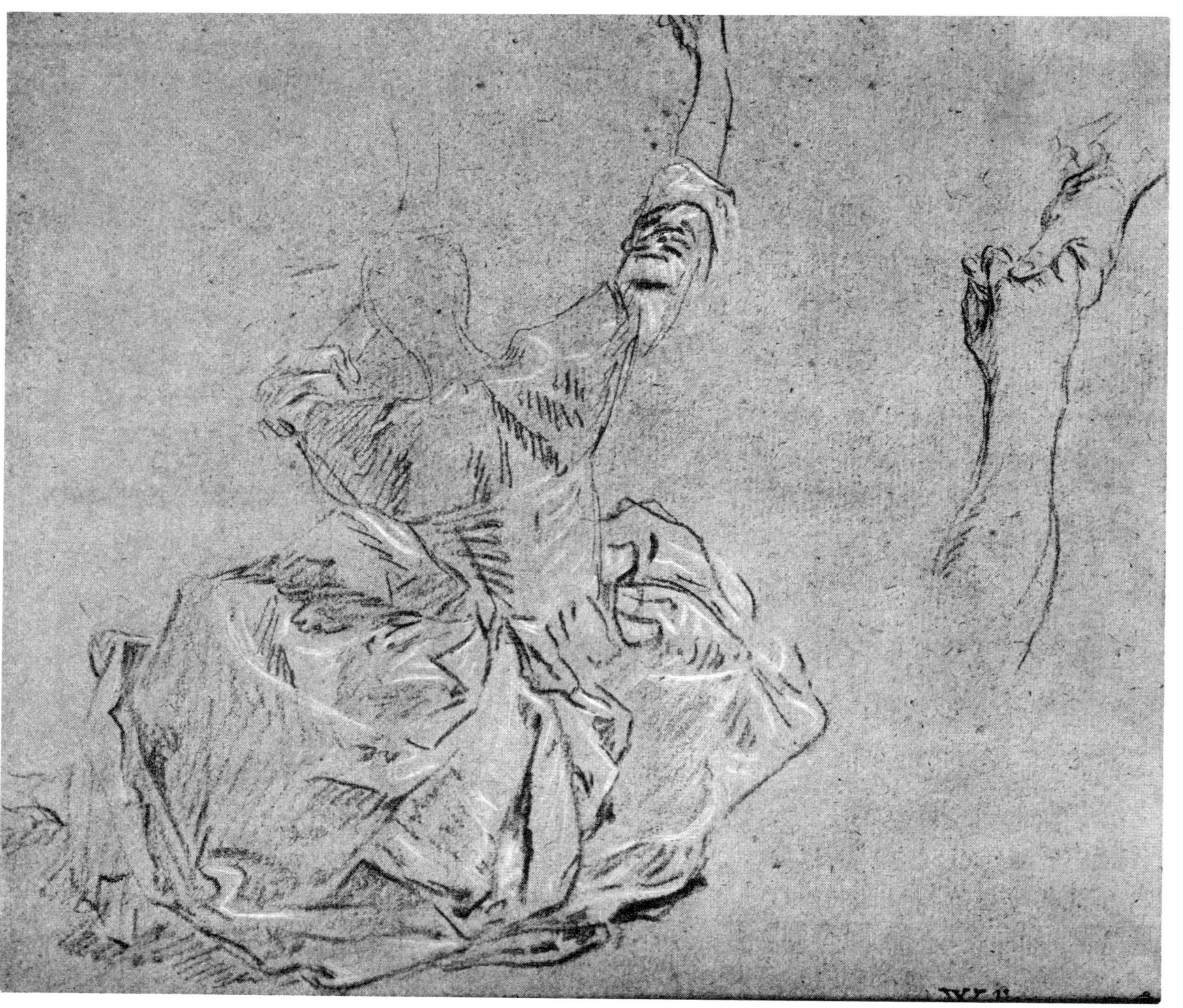

Young woman with raised arms; the hand of a woman in that of a man. Red chalk, white highlights, on brownish-gray paper; 170 × 199 mm.

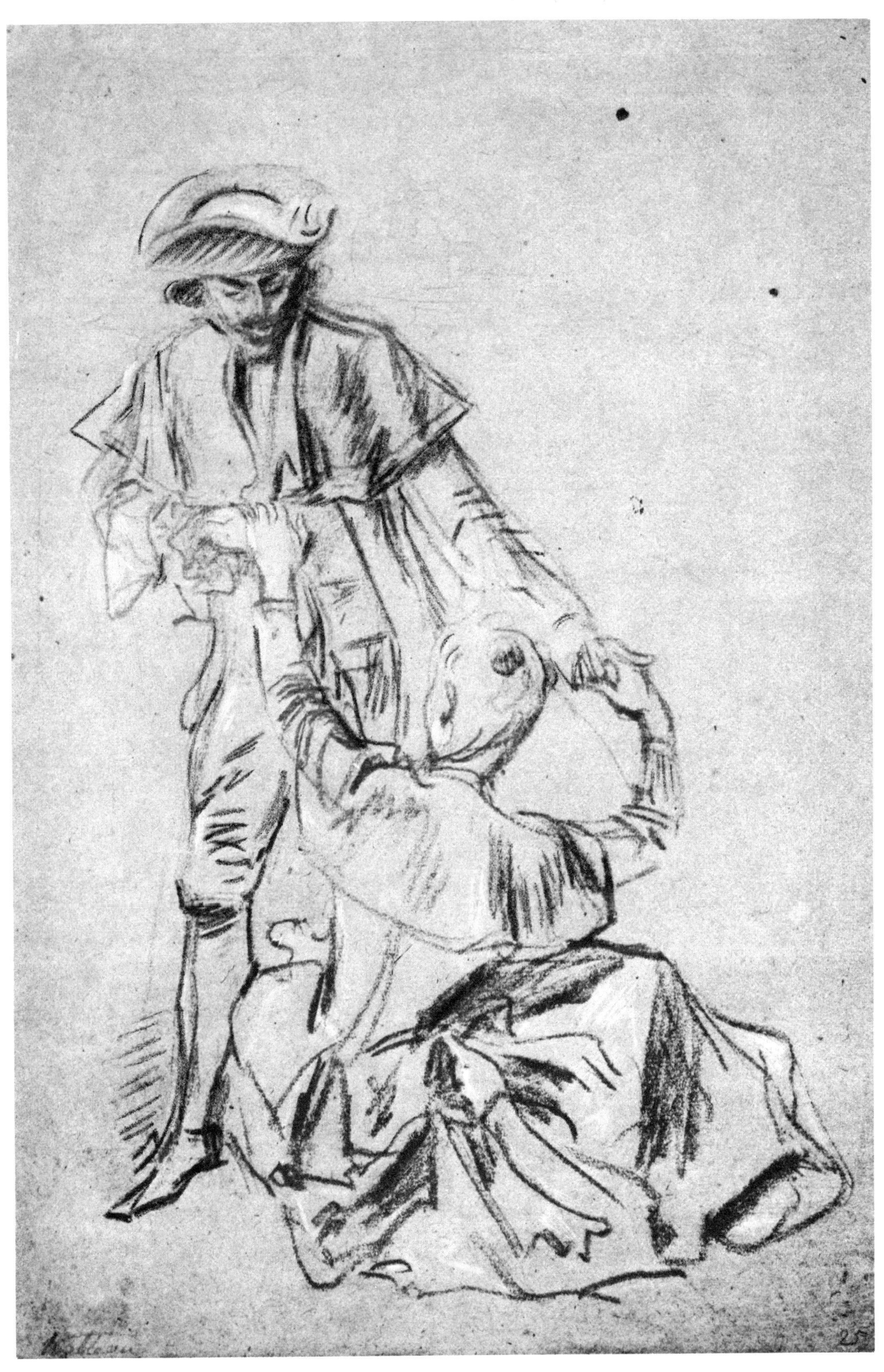

Male pilgrim helping a female pilgrim to her feet. Red, black and white chalk on brown paper; 274 × 182 mm.